WANPHEN HEYMANN-SUKPHAN

THE FOODS OF
THAILAND

*Recipes from the Famous
Sukhothai Restaurant in Zurich*

STEWART, TABORI & CHANG
NEW YORK

Published in 1996 and distributed in the U.S. by
Stewart, Tabori and Chang,
a division of U.S. Media Holdings, Inc.
575 Broadway, New York, NY 10012

Distributed in Canada by General Publishing Co. Ltd.
30 Lesmill Road, Don Mills, Ontario, Canada M3B 2T6
Distributed in Australia and New Zealand by Peribo Pty Ltd.
58 Beaumont Road, Mount Kuring-gai, NSW 2080, Australia
Distributed in all other territories by Grantham Book Services Ltd.
Isaac Newton Way, Alma Park Industrial Estate, Grantham,
Lincs NG31 9SD, England

Photographs by Lottie Bebie
Original German text by Verena Thurner and Monika Schmidhofer
Translation by Angela and Fred Jacobson
Edited by Mary Kalamaras
Designed by Lisa Vaughn

ISBN: 1-55670-457-7

Library of Congress Catalog Card Number: 95-72930

Printed in Hong Kong

10 9 8 7 6 5 4 3 2 1

CONTENTS

About The Author
• 6 •

The Thai Kitchen
• 8 •

Ingredients
• 13 •

Salads
• 30 •

Soups
• 52 •

Curries
• 68 •

Meat & Poultry
• 80 •

Fish & Seafood
• 104 •

Vegetables
• 132 •

Desserts
• 138 •

Basics
• 145 •

Source List
• 149 •

Recipe Index
• 151 •

ABOUT THE AUTHOR

FOODS OF THAILAND

To define Thai cooking is difficult. Actually there is no Thai cooking as such. Every family in Thailand treasures its own recipes, its own kitchen secrets, its own particular variations on the standard fare. Family traditions are preserved in the kitchen. And because in Thailand, as in other countries, traditions are increasingly threatened, numerous recipes have faded from memories. Wanphen Heymann-Sukphan is aware of the importance of preserving her culture's cuisine and has made it her life's work. And she possesses the necessary gifts to do so. She learned to cook under the aegis of her mother and to differentiate between good and bad from her father, a one-time navy cook. She is also blessed with the extraordinary innate ability to determine the ingredients of a dish by smell alone.

At her Sukhothai Restaurant in Zurich, Switzerland, Wanphen has been proving every day of her life that cooking is indeed an art, with an approach that is unique and unmatched. Aficionados claim that Sukhothai has the best Thai food outside of Thailand and Wanphen demonstrates her entitlement to this accolade hour after hour and day after day through her constant discovery of exciting new recipes.

Wanphen runs a kitchen that does not adhere strictly to the printed menu. She knows her steady customers and often cooks especially for them, and because of this, her loyal guests continually return to be pampered and spoiled, sometimes visiting twice in one day. Both her compatriots and luminaries of the world share the same goals: to savor her cooking and her personal warmth.

Harmony is essential to Wanphen, even in the kitchen. She cannot live or cook without a sense of well-being. And it is clearly reflected in the serenity of her face, her shy laugh, and through the skill of her hands as she carves magnificent, filigreed works of art out of fruits and vegetables. The atmosphere and cuisine of Sukhothai is imbued with her essence. She is the spiritual center of her restaurant and it is here that she expresses her family's traditions, creating and testing new recipes and adding them to the hundreds already in her collection. Her devotion to their dissemination is easy to see in the time she spends initiating others in the art of Thai cooking. It is only natural that she now brings to the world her finest recipes, enabling everyone to share in her joy of Thai cooking.

ABOUT THE AUTHOR

THE THAI KITCHEN

Rare is the country whose culinary arts mirror the diversity of its scenery and people as genuinely as does Thailand. It is a land characterized by the magnificence of its beaches, the serenity of its mountainous landscapes, the bustling of its large cities and the majestic beauty of its temples. The lush richness of this landscape, the gentleness of its people with their secretive smile, their unfettered love of food and whole-hearted hospitality are reflected in meals abundant in their charm to bewitch, excite and caress our senses.

Throughout centuries, the people of Thailand have blended their native cooking traditions with the influences of various near and far away neighbors—most notably China, India and Indonesia—yet their culinary art has remained unique. Thai cooking is sometimes described as the Asian version of nouvelle cuisine and the typical Thai table features a bountiful variety of dainty, very thoughtfully prepared delicacies. Meals are often characterized by fiery sauces and artfully carved vegetables and fruit. The tradition of sculpturing vegetables and fruit—an art requiring special dexterity and years of practice—originated in the kitchens of the royal palace where it was the exclusive domain of the ladies in the king's household.

Thai cooking manages to bring together the most diverse spices and aromas—fiery and mild, salty and sweet, sour and bitter—into perfect harmony, not only in each dish, but throughout the entire meal. *Nahm pla,* the fish sauce produced from fish fermented with salt, is indispensable to Thai cooking. Appreciated by the ancient Romans as *garum,* fish sauce replaces salt and provides dishes with an unmistakable intense spiciness. Other spices include shrimp paste, fiery Thai chilies, fragrant Thai basil, lemon grass, peppermint, cilantro, kaffir lime leaves, galangal roots and mild coconut milk. Of these, the hellishly spicy chili introduced to Thailand by the Portuguese in the 16th century is the most important spice. Rice, always served with meals, stays on the table until the very last course. Repasts traditionally end with a selection of fresh fruits such as mangoes, papayas, pineapple, rambutan fruit, or litchi nuts.

Incidentally, Thais eat using a fork and a large spoon. The large spoon can help catch sauces, while a fork is useful in mixing and pushing food onto the spoon. Knives are not required since meat, fish and vegetables are cut into bite-sized pieces prior to cooking.

THE THAI KITCHEN

ABOUT THE RECIPES

GENERAL NOTES:

All recipes are designed to serve four.

Most of the recipes in this book call for the use of a mortar and pestle and it is a good idea to invest in one. Nothing can quite replace this traditional tool for bringing out the full aroma and flavor of ingredients such as lemon grass, cilantro root, galangal root and garlic. However, if necessary, you may substitute with a garlic press or food processor.

You will find that some recipe ingredients list a range in quantity rather than a specific measurement. This is because Thai cooking is extremely flexible, and in experimenting with it, you are encouraged to use herbs and spices according to your own taste preferences. You can be as creative as you desire. Remember only to avoid quantities that may overpower, since the composition of a Thai dish should be balanced.

INGREDIENT NOTES:

Make sure to wash all vegetables, meats and seafoods prior to use.

Marinating meats or seafood should be kept refrigerated until ready to use.

Thai herbs and vegetables differ from their Western counterparts and are singular in taste. Whenever possible, try to shop at a market that imports them directly from Thailand.

If prawns are not available, you may substitute jumbo shrimp. The quantity of 4–8 listed in most of the recipes is dependent upon the size of the prawn. Apportion at least 1/4 pound of seafood per serving.

It is preferred that beef stock be used in recipes calling for stock since it imparts a stronger flavor to Thai dishes. However, if you prefer, you may substitute chicken, lamb, or in the case of seafood recipes, fish stock.

When handling chilies, be especially careful to keep hands away from eyes and mouth and to wash hands thoroughly after handling. If desired, chilies may be seeded to reduce their heat. If not readily available, Thai chilies may be substituted with serrano or jalapeño chilies.

Use sugar (preferably palm sugar) to offset salty and bitter flavors.

Use salt sparingly since fish sauce, used in almost every dish, is sufficiently salty.

In the case where two or more ingredients are combined together—such as fish sauce, lime juice, sugar or oyster sauce—and a measurement is not listed, it is your own taste preference which will determine the resulting balance of sweet, salty and/or sour. Seasoning in proportioned and gradual amounts will allow you to successfully achieve desired taste.

PRONUNCIATION NOTES:

Since Thai is a tonal language with many different dialects, transliteration—the process of representing the letters or words of one language by using the letters or words of another —varies greatly. When an *h* follows a consonant, it is designed to soften the word. For example, *phat* is not meant to be pronounced as *fat*. This spelling instead represents a longer and breathier pronunciation of *pot*.

Unfortunately, transliteration of Thai can only approximate true Thai pronunciation.

1NGREDIENTS

Bamboo

One of Asia's most popular vegetables, bamboo sprouts are the young shoots that grow out of the roots of tropical bamboo grasses (the *phyllostachy, bambusa* and *dendrocalamus* are principal varieties). Like asparagus, the sprouts are cut when their ball-like tips emerge at the surface. At this stage, the sprouts are still tender, light and soft on the inside. If allowed, sprouts can grow into bushes or even trees up to 90 feet high, yielding durable ligneous material for housing and bridge construction and for manufacturing furniture, household appliances and paper.

Fairly neutral in taste, bamboo sprouts are more valued for their crunchiness and the bright color accent they contribute to various dishes. Although they contain few nutrients, they do have a high level of silicic acid, an effective remedy against nervousness.

To maximize flavor, always buy fresh, untrimmed whole bamboo sprouts. To prepare, trim the tips of fresh sprouts, remove their dark outer leaves, cut the ends and cook for 5-10 minutes until tender but still crunchy. If fresh sprouts are not available, cooked and canned sprouts can be found in many supermarkets. Bamboo sprouts can keep fresh up to one week in opened cans, or in sealable glass or plastic containers. However, make sure they remained covered with water that is changed daily.

Banana Flowers

There are two types of banana flowers. The female flower of the banana tree develops into the familiar banana fruit we know, while at the end of the flower stalk, its male counterpart develops into a cob-shaped fruit that is very popular in Asia. This fruit can reach lengths of up to 2 feet and has a slightly sour taste, similar to raw artichokes. It is used primarily in soups and fish dishes.

To prepare, remove the red-leaved husk and trim the stem back. Cook whole with several lemon slices in boiling, salted water for 15-20 minutes. Cut into thin slices. Halve slices if too large in size.

Prepared as described, the fruit can also be eaten like an artichoke, stripped leaf by leaf for dunking in a seasoned sauce.

Banana flowers are generally found only in well-stocked Asian food stores.

Basil

Thai cooking relies on three different types of basil. Botanically, *bai horapha* (*ocimum basilicum*) is identical to our commonly known basil except for the bluntness of its leaves, a more intensive taste and an anise fragrance. *Bai manglak* (*ocimum carnum*), used generously in curries, salads and soups, is light green in color and its leaves are speckled with hair. *Bai Krapao* (*ocimum sanctum*) is distinguished by violet-reddish stems and a strong zesty flavor with a slight medicinal taste.

Thai basil can be found Asian food shops but, if necessary, may be substituted with European or local basil. It can also be grown at home providing it is exposed to a warm and sunny climate.

Celery

Celery's distinct taste is derived from etheric oil, the celery oil. This plant is rich with mineral salts and vitamins and known for its diuretic and digestive effects.

Thai cooks prefer using finely-cut celery and very tender celery sticks in their cooking, incorporating both its leaves and roots.

Dishes including large quantities of celery require less salt.

Chilies

....

Chili peppers (*capsicummannuum var. frutescens*)—belong to the paprika family and were brought to the Old World by Spanish conquerors of Central and Latin America. Chilies give Thai cooking its fiery bite and intensity. Used in countless dishes, this vegetable is basic to chili pastes and, therefore, to classic curries as well.

Rich in vitamin C and an aid to digestion, chili peppers come in all varieties, shapes and colors. Small birds-eye chilies are the most pungent. Larger-sized peppers have a lesser bite, as in the jalapeño chili pepper.

Although using fresh chilies is preferred in Thai cooking, they are also available in dry flake and powder forms. Dried varieties are more spirited in flavor than fresh and, like fresh chilies, the smaller they are, the more fiery. Dried chilies can be used like fresh after being soaked in warm water for about 15 minutes.

It is recommended to use chili peppers with caution at first, then carefully adjusting quantities to desired spiciness. The "burning" effect can be reduced by removing the partitioning walls and seeds of the chili. Always wash hands immediately after handling.

Chili Oil

....

For spice and taste sprinkle only a few drops of chili oil on a dish before serving. This oil, sold ready-to-use in specialty stores, can also be made at home. Roast dry, red chilies in vegetable oil or peanut oil and strain. Chili oil will keep for several months if stored in a cool, dry place.

Chili Paste

....

Chili paste is a thick mass of spices consisting of chilies, garlic and seasoning and forms the basis for classic curries and many spicy sauces and dishes. Thai cooking features four basic chili paste preparations: *red curry paste, green curry paste, Massaman curry paste* and *Panaeng curry paste* (see recipes, pages 146–147).

Chili paste can be prepared for use at a later date. Refrigerated, it keeps for up to a week. Larger quantities can be frozen in portions. Quality chili pastes are also available in Asian specialty stores.

Chinese Broccoli

....

Chinese broccoli (*brassica alboglabra*), common in Thailand, is as closely related to the cabbage family as its Western counterpart, although distinctly different in configuration and taste. The plant grows to a height of three feet. However, instead of little flower panicles, or florets, it has hearty, meaty stems with dense, robust leaves. The stems, which taste very much like chard and are used in the same way, are trimmed and cut into bite-sized pieces.

Chinese broccoli can be substituted by well-trimmed Western broccoli stems.

Chinese Mushrooms

....

The *tongu* mushroom *(lentinus edodes)*, known in Japanese as *shiitake,* is a very popular tree mushroom in Asia. Like the dark meadow (*Champignon*) mushroom, the tongu has a thick, meaty cap with a hairy pattern on top and a thin, tough stalk. To intensify taste, these mushrooms are usually dried. Prior to use, soak Chinese mushrooms for 1–2 hours in cold water, then rinse thoroughly under cold running water. If pressed for time, soak in warm water for 20-30 minutes. Do not use stalks.

The Chinese *mu-err* mushroom (*auricularia polytricha*), black in color, also grows on tree trunks or is cultivated on wood. Available only in dried form, the tough and spongy mushroom must also first be soaked (see directions above). Make sure the water is changed frequently. This mushroom variety swells to many times its dried size.

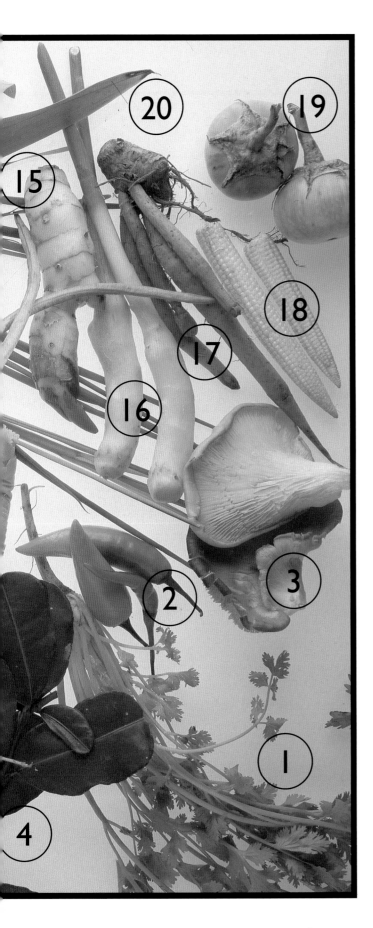

1	Cilantro (Coriander)
2	Chilies
3	Oyster Mushrooms
4	Kaffir Lime Leaves
5	Bamboo Shoots
6	Banana Flower
7	Chinese Broccoli
8	Celery
9	Sour Mango
10	Green Papaya
11	Thai Basil
12	Satow Bean
13	Lemon Grass
14	Yard-Long Beans
15	Galangal Root
16	Ginger Root (young)
17	Krachai Root
18	Baby Corn
19	Thai Eggplant
20	Pandan Leaf
21	Spring Onions
22	Chinese Watercress
23	Shaom

INGREDIENTS

When considering a substitution, be aware that many tree mushrooms are not good substitutes for Chinese mushrooms as their flavors are not as intense.

Chinese Watercress

The Chinese watercress plant is related to the once exclusively European watercress (*nasturtium officinale*), now found throughout the world. This plant's root system grows along the bottom of ponds and brooks and its stems rise above the water's surface, sprouting round leaves. While the Chinese variety shares the similar fresh, peppery taste of its European counterpart, it differs in appearance and is characterized by longer, narrow leaves.

In the Western world, watercress is commonly used as an herb or as part of a tasty salad mix. In Asia, the entire plant is usually fried and served as a vegetable accompaniment.

According to folklore, watercress is said to have genuine magical powers. Its juice supposedly cleanses the stomach, enhances the skin and complexion and brightens eyes. It acts as a diuretic, cleansing the blood and alleviating kidney, spleen and liver ailments. According to scientific fact, the plant, does indeed, contains extraordinarily high levels of vitamins and minerals—far greater than in other salad greens—as well as some sulfur, iodine and substances with antibiotic qualities.

Chinese watercress can be found in well-stocked Asian specialty stores.

Cilantro

Cilantro (*coriandrum sativum*), also known as *coriander* and *Chinese parlsey*, is an herb with a 3,000 year history that originated in the Mediterranean and Caucasus and is, today, widely cultivated. Cilantro belongs to the *umbelliferae* family and is a relative of the carrot. It features a striped stem and small white or pink flowers and its intense spiciness is derived from etheric oil.

Cilantro is indispensable in Thai cooking. Fresh, green cilantro leaves are used both as a flavoring and a garnish. Thais incorporate the roots as well, crushing and combining them in a mortar together with other ingredients. The seeds, more familiarly known as the coriander spice, are crushed and used in curries and curry pastes.

Fresh cilantro has become increasingly available, however parsley roots can be substituted if necessary. Cilantro stems can be substituted for roots that may have been trimmed off prior to purchase.

The cilantro plant is an annual and can be grown from seeds. The kernels should be planted loosely between March and April, covered thinly with soil, exposed to light, and kept humid and warm until they sprout.

Coconut

Like bamboo, the coconut palm is a major tropical crop. The trunk, leaves and fiber hull of the mature fruit are used as construction, roofing and insulating materials or processed into brooms, cord, wicker goods and mats. The juice extracted from the flowers becomes palm sugar or, by way of fermentation and distillation, palm wine or brandy (*Arrack*).

As a food, the coconut has many different uses in Thai cooking. When still young, the fruit with its shiny, slightly pale meat, is valued for the refreshing, flavorful water found at its center. Coconut oil, milk, flakes and fillings, however, can only be procured from the white, fatty meat of the mature fruit.

Coconut milk—not to be confused with the water of the young fruit—is prepared by pouring boiling water over freshly-grated pulp, letting it stand 15-20 minutes, then straining and pressing the pulp. This process yields a thick, cream-like coconut milk with a high fat content (also referred to as coconut cream) which can often be found on the surface of canned coconut milk. A second pouring of hot water over the pulp produces a thinner coconut milk which is principally used in soups.

When buying canned coconut milk, take care to select the unsweetened variety.

Dried Prawns

In Thailand, as in many other countries, drying fish and seafood by salting, then exposing to the sun, is a traditional approach to preserving and creates a strong and concentrated taste.

In their sun-dried form, prawns are a key ingredient to Thai sauces, curries and salads. Preparation is simple, involving finely crushing the dried prawns by hand or with a mortar and pestle.

Dried prawns can be found in Asian specialty stores.

Durian

Despite its very foul-smelling odor, the fruit of the durian tree is extremely popular in Asia, affording a simultaneously spicy and fruity taste, quite alien to Western palates. The durian fruit has a pale yellow, spiky skin, edible seeds and soft meat, and can sometimes weigh up to 18 pounds. It is incorporated in both sweet and savory Thai dishes.

Fish Sauce

Referred to as *nuoc* in Vietnamese and *nahm pla* in Thai, fish sauce is as common a condiment in Thai cooking as salt is to Western cooking. Similar to *garum*, an Indian spice, fish sauce is made from fish and prawns that have been fermented in salt. The resulting light-brown sauce is clear in texture and penetrating in its spiciness. Its distinctive flavor is present in practically all Thai dishes, especially salads. Use this salty condiment sparingly, and take care not to season the dish with any additional salt.

Eggplant

Like the tomato, eggplant (or aubergine) is a member of the nightshade family. Originating in India, it has, since the Middle Ages, also become indigenous to the Mediterranean region.

Besides the common, large, dark-violet fruit known to Westerners, eggplants come in slender, long shapes in snow-white, light green or striped colors, or in small, round and oval varieties that are green, yellow or white. All of these varieties can be traced back to an original eggplant variety the size and color of a chicken egg; thus, the name "eggplant."

The popularity of eggplant in Thailand is reflected in the widespread use of it in a variety of fish, meat and curry dishes, as well as in salads and as an accompaniment to fillings. The meat and seeds of the eggplant, if fresh, are always white. Eggplant can only be kept for a limited time and should be stored separately because it reacts to the ethylene emitted by any surrounding fruits or vegetables.

If the desired small Thai eggplant is not available, another variety may be easily substituted.

Galangal

Galangal, also known as *Siamese ginger*, is the type of ginger most popular in Thai cooking. Long known to Egyptians as an effective purifier and valued by medieval Europeans as a healing agent and spice, galangal, is now grown and used mainly in India and southeast Asia.

Unlike common ginger, galangal has larger and more translucent roots. The root tips are pink and have a severe medicinal taste reminiscent of a combination of ginger and pepper with a touch of lemon. In Thai cooking, galangal is an important ingredient in soups, particularly the famous *Tom Yum Goong*.

The medicinal effects of this root are still being exploited in Asia, especially for the treatment of

• 19 •

FOODS OF THAILAND

1.   Pineapple

2.   Coconut (Trimmed)

3   Thai Bananas

4.   Papaya

5.   Mango

6.   Litchi Nuts

7.   Mangosteen Fruit

8.   Rambutan Fruit

catarrh, respiratory disorders and indigestion.

Galangal roots are available fresh, dried and in powder form from Asian groceries. If necessary, common ginger can be substituted but the taste of the dish will be altered. Wrapped in a damp towel, fresh galangal roots can either be kept refrigerated for two to three weeks or stored in the freezer.

Garlic

Garlic, one of the oldest known herbs, is believed to have originated in southwest Asia, where it thrives under the hot, dry climate. Reputed to have numerous health benefits, garlic is believed to prevent infections, stimulate blood circulation and digestion, to contribute to lower blood pressure and cholesterol levels and to deter constriction and calcification of blood vessels. Whether for health or taste reasons, chopped, ground, crushed into paste, or fried crisp, garlic is used liberally in Thai cooking.

Light red-violet in color and milder in taste, Thai garlic cloves are distinctly smaller than other garlic cloves. However, if tender and fresh, the common Western variety can be used.

Ginger

Grown in tropical Asia for more than 3,000 years, ginger (*zingiber officinale*) is one of the first and most important Asian spices to reach the Mediterranean region. By the 9th century, ginger was a familiar staple spice to the ancient Egyptians, Greeks and Romans.

Ginger is recognized as a stimulant for the stomach and a promoter of digestion. Ginger tea is said to enhance blood circulation. In Thai cooking, numerous dishes owe their flavor to the fruitiness and spiciness of ginger. It is best to rely on fresh, young ginger, which is delicate and mild in taste. The root bulb should be firm and juicy, the skin white-beige, silky and shiny.

Ginger root is available fresh, dried, or ground as a

preserve. When fresh, ginger can be kept for two to three weeks in the refrigerator if wrapped in a moist cloth. To conveniently freeze: peel, finely chop and store the pieces in a shallow container.

Glass Noodles

Glass noodles are also known as *Chinese noodles* or *cellophane noodles*. These long, very fine noodles, are made from the flour of green mung beans. Slippery-smooth and neutral in taste, glass noodles absorb all spices and flavors well. They are used in soups and meat and vegetable dishes.

Prior to use, soak noodles in hot water for about 5 minutes, during which time the noodles will become transparent. Since the strands in commercial noodle varieties are very long, cut them into manageable lengths after soaking.

Kaffir Lime

Lemons are not part of the Thailand cuisine, it is the lime, instead, that is the commonly used citrus fruit. The Kaffir lime (*citrushysterix*) is smaller than the Western lime and is covered by a thick, dark, wrinkled skin. Its leaves and peel are the parts used in Thai cooking. Similar to lemon grass, Kaffir lime leaves have a strong lemon flavor and add to the incomparable freshness and clarity of taste in Thai dishes.

The leaves of this lime are firm to the touch, shiny, lush green in color and grow in pairs on the stem, one behind the other. They are a popular ingredient and can either be sliced very thinly, or lightly pounded with a kitchen mallet until soft in texture. The thick, knobby and wrinkled skin of the fruit can also be cooked to add flavor to dishes.

Lime leaves are available fresh or dried in Asian food stores. Like lemon grass, fresh leaves can be kept longer by freezing. If necessary, lime or lemon peel or lemon grass may be substituted

Krachai Root

Krachai root (*kaempferia pandurata*), is another popular and important root spice used in Thai cooking, along with ginger and galangal roots. Krachai root is long, thin, finger-like and has a brown skin. Milder in taste than ginger or galangal, the roots are finely chopped, then fried or boiled giving dishes an appealing yellow hue.

Lemon Grass

This tough, reed-like plant (*Cymbopogon citratus*), which grows up to three feet tall, gets its name from the strong lemon aroma it releases when its greenish-white bulbous base is finely ground. In contrast, the green stalks are used less frequently for this purpose. Lemon grass can also be finely chopped, or squeezed and then cooked with food, but it should be removed before eating.

Prior to using lemon grass, remove the tough outer stalks and trim the roots. Lemon grass may be obtained fresh or dried in Asian specialty stores. Since it can keep well for a long time when frozen, it is advisable to obtain large quantities of it when it becomes available. If necessary, the peel of a lemon which has not been chemically sprayed may be substituted.

Litchi Nut

This fruit, which originated in south China, is covered by a thin, leathery, spiny, or knobby rose to red-colored shell. When ripe, the litchi nut is strong-scented, very juicy, sweet and flavorful.

Litchi nuts are also available canned.

Mango

Mango, India's national fruit, has been cultivated for more than 4,000 years and today ranks as one of the most important fruits in the tropics. Ranging from apricot sized to an amazing four pounds in weight, mangoes come in a variety of colors and shapes.

The popularity of the mango is probably attributable to its delicate peach-like flesh when ripe. In tropical climates mango is also eaten, like papaya, in its unripened, green state. The refreshing and tart flesh of this "sour mango" is used in salads or cooked as a vegetable. To quell thirst, Thais eat pieces of sour mango sprinkled with sugar and dried chili.

Mangosteen

Unrelated to the mango and native to Malaysia, this fist-sized fruit has a thick, leathery, dark-violet to purple non-edible skin. The white flesh of the fruit is soft, juicy and sweet-sour in taste and easily divisible into segments. The fruit should only be eaten fresh since its quality rapidly deteriorates during storage. Once its shell hardens, the mangosteen is usually no longer edible.

When conserved in syrup, mangosteens differ greatly from their fresh counterparts.

Mushrooms

See oyster mushrooms, Chinese mushrooms

Nuts

Crunchy, crispy nuts like cashews and peanuts are a favored ingredient for various stir-fried dishes, curries and salads. Chicken dishes, especially, benefit from the addition of cashew nuts.

1	Panaeng Curry Paste
2	Green Curry Paste
3	Massaman Curry Paste
4	Red Curry Paste
5	Cashew Nuts
6	Palm Sugar
7	Chinese Dried Mushrooms
8	Dried Shrimp
9	Large Dried Thai Chilies
10	Small Dried Thai Chilies
11	Green Rice
12	Tapioca Flour
13	Sticky Rice
14	Aromatic Rice
15	Spaghetti from Rice Flour
16	Glass Noodles
17	Rice Noodles
18	Coconut Milk
19	Fish Sauce
20	Light Soy Sauce
21	Oyster Sauce
22	Soybeans

INGREDIENTS

If at all possible, use fresh, unroasted and unsalted nuts. If only salted nuts are available, scrape away all the salt before using.

Oyster Mushroom

The oyster mushroom (*pleurotus ostreatus*), which grows wild on deciduous trees, is distinguished by a dove-gray cap and a mild, unremarkable flavor. Oyster mushrooms are added to numerous dishes and soups. Other mushroom varieties may be substituted.

Oyster Sauce

Dark, viscous and salty, oyster sauce is made from cooking oysters in brine and soy sauce. Used in many stir-fried dishes, oyster sauce not only seasons food but also imparts to it a sea-like aroma. It is available ready made.

Palm Sugar

Palm sugar, also known as *jaggery*, is an unrefined, coarse brown sugar derived from the sap of coconut and palmyra palms, then cooked into a light-colored translucent syrup and allowed to crystalize. Used as a sweetener, it has a distinct malt taste. If the sap is not cooked immediately, it begins to ferment and becomes palm wine (*toddy*), which, when distilled, becomes palm brandy, also known as *arrack*.

If palm sugar is not available, brown sugar can be used instead.

Pandan Leaves

The art of packaging and wrapping food in the leaves of various plants is part of traditional Thai and other Asian cooking practices. Leaves are a natural packing material, used in markets by street vendors and at roadside eateries. Leaves are also used as a protective wrap for cooking delicate fish or meat. The long, narrow leaves of the pandan plant are especially popular. A member of the *pandanaceae* family, it is also known also as *screw pine* or *pandang*. Pandan leaves, though not consumed, have a fine aroma and the subtlety of their spice permeates the food they contain.

Although they lack the corresponding flavor, banana leaves may be substituted. If not available, parchment paper or aluminum foil will suffice.

Papaya

Papaya, now native throughout the world's tropical areas, originated in Central America and was brought to the Philippines by 16th-century seafarers.

In contrast to the small papaya of the West, the Thai variety weighs between two to four pounds. Like the mango, unripe papaya is used in its native tropics in salads and as a vegetable. Its taste is roughly similar to a combination of strawberry and peach flavors. The flesh of the papaya is juicy, sweet, yellow to rose-red or orange-red in color. Rich in vitamins and minerals, it is regarded as a detoxifier and an aid to digestion. The milk-juice of the papaya is laced with papain, an enzyme which has multiple uses in medicine.

Ripe papaya tastes best when sprinkled with a few drops of lime juice.

Pepper

Pepper, now a common spice, was once so highly coveted and treasured that it was treated as currency.

In addition to familiar ground and milled whole peppercorns, Thai cooking also incorporates the plant's panicles that still bearing the fresh, immature, small peppercorns. Although somewhat less sharp, they have a fresher taste. Green peppercorns are also available dried or preserved in brine or vinegar.

Pineapple

Thailand is a major producer and exporter of pineapples (also known as *ananas*). The fruit is served fresh, consumed as juice and featured in many recipes. Its yellow, fibrous and juicy flesh is valued not only for its minerals and high sugar content, but also for the bromelin it contains, an agent that promotes digestion.

Prawn Paste

Prawn paste varies from red to violet to brown in color and is known in Thai as *khapi*. Derived from air-dried prawns this slightly salty paste and its robust sea aroma is the ingredient of many curries and sauces.

Prawn paste, obtainable in Asian specialty stores, can be substituted with anchovy paste.

Rambutan

Related to the litchi nut, the rambutan is a plum-sized fruit with dark red skin and long red and yellow bristles. Its flesh is milky-white, sweet and flavorful, but because it cannot be preserved for long, the fruit is difficult to export and, for that reason, is scarce in the West.

Rice

Rice is Thailand's most important food staple, grown in ample quantities throughout the country and exported worldwide. Of the varieties, aromatic rice is is the most popular and served with all meals. True to its name, this long-grain variety has a marvelous aroma. The short grains of this sticky rice bond tightly together after cooking and appear to have a glassy shimmer. Sticky rice is also used in desserts.

Green rice, also a dessert rice, is aromatized with fermented pandan leaves.

Rice Noodles

Made from rice flour, these noodles come in shapes ranging from very thin, to flat strips, and in widths from one half to two centimeters. Prior to cooking, they should be soaked in warm water for about 20 minutes.

Satow Beans

Satow beans are Thailand's version of the European broad bean and available only in Thailand. Satow bean pods are long, green and broad, resembling lima or fava beans. and only their seeds are consumed. Although no substitute can quite match them, they can be substituted with fresh, young fava beans, fresh lima beans, or fresh sugar-snap or snow peas.

Shaom

Shaom, or *Cha-om*, is the Thai name for the locust tree (*acacia pennata var. insuavis*). Its offshoots are cultivated into vegetable plants in central Thailand and take a year to develop into young sprouts with a delicate, thorny plummage. Subtle, yet spicy in flavor, shaom contains protein and carbohydrates and is rich in minerals and vitamin C.

Shaom is available only in Asian foodstores.

Sour Mango

See mango

Soy Sauce

Soy sauce, a condiment generally associated with Chinese and Japanese cooking, is made from fermented soybeans, barley, toasted wheat, salt and water. Except for its use in the ever-popular fish sauce, it plays somewhat of a subordinate role in Thai cooking. When it is called for in a dish, it is preferable to use light soy sauce rather than dark soy sauce. Light soy sauce is light in color and subtle in flavor and not to be confused with "lite" or low salt soy sauce.

Spring Onions/Scallions

Spring onions (scallions/green onions) are any young, immature onions that have been harvested with their green shoots. Despite their name they are available throughout the year. In Thai cooking, both the white bulb and the green shoots are used generously and in a number of ways: cooked, steamed, stir-fried in a variety of dishes, or used raw for decorating or sprinkling over soups and salads.

Tapioca

Like arrowroot flour, tapioca is made from the starch-bearing tropical cassava root. Snow-white and neutral in taste, it thickens less than corn starch but does not produce cloudiness and is therefore ideally suited to bind clear soups and sauces. Tapioca is available in the form of flour, flakes, or pearls (sago).

Corn starch is a good substitute for tapioca.

Thai Bananas

Banana trees originated in southeast Asia and date back thousands of years. Records of Chinese banana plantations date back as far as the year 200 B.C.

Among the many varieties of bananas available, Thais prefer the small, finger-length fruits which are much softer and sweeter than the bananas familiar to the West.

Yard-Long Beans

This plant (*Vigna unguiculata ssp. sesquipedalis*), native to southern Asia, owes its name to the fact it can grow up to three feet long, yet also goes by the names *Chinese long bean*, *asparagus bean*, *string bean*, or *snake bean*.

Yard-long beans do not have to be stringed and they cook faster and are somewhat sweeter than the Western garden variety. However, regular green beans may easily be substituted.

RECIPES

SALADS

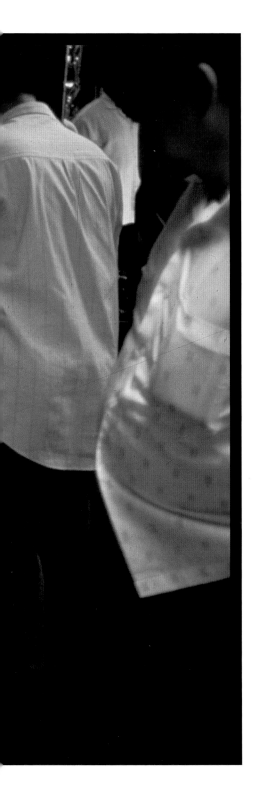

Thais call salad *yum*, literally meaning "to mix with the hands." The word also connotes the country's wonderfully diverse approach to food preparation. A Thai salad may feature fish, seafood, stir-fried meat, poultry, noodles, or fruits. Market-fresh vegetables like cucumbers, red peppers, spring onions, beans, tomatoes, celery, carrots and onions also play an important role. Thai salads are generously seasoned with fresh herbs: peppermint, lime leaves, basil and, of course, all-important cilantro. Spice is provided by pungent, small Thai chilies, dried shrimp, peanuts and garlic. Thai salads are almost always topped with a delicately balanced combination of fish sauce, sugar and lime juice and served on seasonal greens.

In Thailand, salads are not intended merely to stimulate appetites in preparation for the main course, nor are they considered just a frill or simply a source of vitamins. Salads are as indispensable to the Thai menu. Indeed, by virtue of their ingredients, they can even compete with the entrée.

During the day *yum* is an important pick-me-up. Nothing refreshes more in the heat of the day or sustains the body better than a magnificent Thai salad. In the evening when Thais eat their one and only major meal, *yum* is again part of the menu along with soup, meat and fish dishes. *Yum* exposes the senses to the delights of Thai dishes and demonstrates the richness and uniqueness of the nation's exotic culinary expressions.

PRAWN SALAD

Yum Goong

Shell prawns, halve lengthwise and devein. Cook in hot water until just pink. Remove and allow to cool. Roll up lime leaves and cut into thin slices. Thinly slice lemon grass and shallot. Cut red pepper and cucumber into bite-sized pieces. Set aside.

Combine fish sauce, lime juice and sugar and heat briefly until sugar dissolves. Set aside to cool. Cut prawns into small pieces and toss with lime leaves, lemon grass, red pepper and cucumber. Top with cooled sauce and sprinkle with peppermint leaves. Garnish with thinly-sliced chilies.

• 32 •

• • • • • • • • • • • • • •

4 to 8 prawns
2 fresh Kaffir lime leaves
1 stalk lemon grass
1 shallot
1 red bell pepper
1/2 cucumber
2 tbsp. fish sauce
3 tbsp. lime juice
1 to 2 tbsp. sugar
peppermint leaves, to taste
fresh chilies, for garnish

S A L A D S

SOUR MANGO SALAD WITH CRAYFISH

Yum Goong Talay Mamuang

S lit open crayfish shells lengthwise on each side and remove meat. Coat with fish sauce. Combine 2 tablespoons fish sauce, lime juice and sugar and heat briefly until sugar dissolves. Set aside to cool.

Cut red pepper, cucumber and tomatoes into small pieces and finely slice lemon grass. Coarsely chop lettuce leaves and toss together with red pepper, cucumber, tomatoes, lemon grass and soybean sprouts. Peel mangoes and cut into fine strips. Mix in with other salad ingredients and top with cooled sauce.

Sauté crayfish in vegetable oil until golden brown. Drain on paper towels, then arrange over salad.

• • • • • • • • • • • • • •

4 to 6 crayfish
fish sauce, to taste
2 tbsp. fish sauce
2 tbsp. lime juice
1 tbsp. sugar
1 red bell pepper
1/2 cucumber
1 to 2 tomatoes
1 stalk lemon grass
1 head of lettuce
   (Boston or iceberg)
1 handful fresh soybean sprouts
1 to 2 sour mangoes
vegetable oil, for frying

S A L A D S

FRESH SQUID SALAD

Yum Pla Muk

Rinse each squid thoroughly under cold, running water. Peel skin and discard along with tentacles, head and innards. Remove and discard transparent cuttlebone. Rinse remaining bodies thoroughly, cut each in half and place flat on a cutting board. With a sharp knife, score a large cross-cut into each squid piece. Briefly blanch pieces in boiling water, then plunge immediately into cold water. Drain and set aside.

Thinly slice shallots, chop celery and cut up cucumber. Cut the white portion of spring onions into 3/4-inch pieces and slice green stalks into thin rolls. Combine fish sauce, lime juice and sugar and heat briefly until sugar dissolves. Set aside to cool.

Mix squid and all vegetables together and sprinkle with cooled sauce. Add finely-chopped chili to taste. Arrange on lettuce leaves and garnish with peppermint and cilantro leaves before serving.

• 36 •

• • • • • • • • • • • • • •

8 fresh young squid

2 shallots

1 to 2 celery ribs

1/2 cucumber

2 spring onions or scallions

2 tbsp. fish sauce

2 tbsp. lime juice

1 tbsp. sugar

1 chili

fresh leaf lettuce

peppermint leaves, for garnish

cilantro leaves, for garnish

SALADS

SPICY TUNA SALAD

Yum Pla

Cut tuna into bite-sized pieces, coat with fish sauce and panfry briefly in very hot vegetable oil. Combine fish sauce, lime juice and sugar and heat briefly until sugar dissolves. Set aside to cool.

Quarter tomatoes and mince shallot. Cut white portion of spring onions into 3/4-inch pieces and slice green stalks into thin rolls. Slice chilies. Pick cilantro and basil leaves from sprigs. Toss tomatoes, shallot, onions, chilies, cilantro leaves and basil leaves together in a bowl. Add cooled sauce and mix well. Arrange salad on lettuce leaves and garnish with lukewarm tuna pieces before serving.

● ● ● ● ● ● ● ● ● ● ● ● ● ● ●

1 1/3 lb fresh tuna
fish sauce, to taste
vegetable oil
2 tbsp. fish sauce
2 tbsp. lime juice
1 tbsp. sugar
8 cherry tomatoes
1 shallot
5 spring onions or scallions
2 to 3 chilies
1 bunch cilantro
1 bunch Thai basil
fresh leaf lettuce

FRESH OYSTER SALAD

Yum Hoy Naerng Rom

Combine fish sauce, lime juice and sugar and heat briefly until sugar dissolves. Set aside to cool.

Finely slice shallot and spring onions. Coarsely chop garlic. Roll up lime leaves and slice into very thin strips. Thinly slice chilies.

Wash and shuck oysters carefully (discard liquor). Season with fish sauce and panfry briefly in vegetable oil. Toss shallot, onions, garlic, lime leaves, chilies and oysters togther in a bowl and sprinkle with cooled sauce. Arrange on lettuce leaves.

Note: You may substitute clams for oysters.

● ● ● ● ● ● ● ● ● ● ● ● ● ● ●

1 tbsp. fish sauce
2 tbsp. lime juice
1 tsp. sugar
1 shallot
4 to 5 spring onions or scallions
2 to 4 garlic cloves
2 fresh Kaffir lime leaves
2 to 3 small chilies
8 fresh oysters
fish sauce, to taste
2 tbsp. vegetable oil
fresh leaf lettuce

SAUTÉED CHICKEN AND VEGETABLE SALAD

Yum Gai Yang

Season chicken breast with light soy sauce and pepper and fry in ungreased, non-stick skillet until cooked through. When cool enough to handle, cut chicken into bite-sized pieces.

Cut carrots and beans into bite-sized pieces and blanch in boiling water. Cut up cucumber and spring onions. Quarter cherry tomatoes. Arrange chicken onto lettuce leaves along with cut vegetables and soybean sprouts.

To prepare sauce, mince chilies, shallot and garlic and stir-fry in an ungreased non-stick skillet. Transfer to blender and purée. Return to skillet with water and simmer until purée begins to thicken. Season with desired balance of fish sauce, lime juice and sugar. Let sauce cool and serve as a side dip for salad.

● ● ● ● ● ● ● ● ● ● ● ● ● ●
1 1/2 lbs. skinless, boneless
   chicken breast
light soy sauce, to taste
freshly ground pepper, to taste
1 to 2 carrots
3 oz. yard-long beans
1/2 cucumber
2 spring onions or scallions
8 cherry tomatoes
4 oz. soybean sprouts
leaf lettuce

● ● ● ● ● ● ● ● ● ● ● ● ● ●
SAUCE:
2 to 3 yellow chilies
1 shallot
2 to 3 garlic cloves
1 to 2 tbsp. water
fish sauce, to taste
lime juice, to taste
sugar, to taste

• 39 •

SEAFOOD SALAD WITH PORK

Yum Moo Talay

Rinse each squid thoroughly under cold, running water. Peel skin and discard along with tentacles, head and innards. Remove and discard transparent cuttlebone. Rinse remaining bodies thoroughly, cut each in half and place flat on a cutting board. With a sharp knife, score a large cross-cut into each squid piece. Briefly blanch pieces in boiling water, then plunge immediately into cold water.

Shell prawns, halve lengthwise and devein. Coat prawns with fish sauce and sauté in oil until golden brown. Drain on paper towels and set aside.

Finely chop chilies and mince shallot. Sauté pork together with chilies and shallot until cooked through. Season with fish sauce and set aside.

Soak glass noodles in cold water for 10 minutes, then place in a colander and dip briefly into enough boiling water to cover. Remove colander and run noodles under cold, running water. Drain well.

Combine fish sauce, lime juice and sugar and heat briefly until sugar dissolves. Set aside to cool. Cut spring onions into bite-sized pieces and toss with pork and glass noodles in a mixing bowl. Add cooled sauce and season dish to taste. Arrange pork and noodles onto lettuce leaves. Garnish with crayfish, squid and peppermint leaves before serving.

3 fresh young squid

4 to 8 prawns

fish sauce, to taste

vegetable oil

2 to 3 chilies

1 shallot

6 oz. lean ground pork

1/2 package glass noodles

1 tbsp. fish sauce

2 tbsp. lime juice

1 tbsp. sugar

5 spring onions or scallions

fresh leaf lettuce

peppermint leaves, for garnish

SALADS

SPICY CHICKEN SALAD

Lahb Gai

Finely chop chicken breast and lightly stir-fry in an ungreased non-stick skillet until tender. Drizzle with lime juice. Combine fish sauce, lime juice and sugar and heat briefly until sugar dissolves. Set aside to cool.

Dice tomatoes, celery and cucumber and thinly slice bell peppers. Finely chop shallots, spring onions and garlic cloves. Slice chilies. Mix chicken and cut vegetables together well. Add sesame seeds, chili paste and chili flakes.

To serve, sprinkle cooled sauce over salad and toss well. Fill hollow bell peppers with salad and garnish with peppermint leaves.

Note: Quantities of each vegetable can be varied according to preference.

• • • • • • • • • • • •

10 oz. boneless, skinless chicken breast

2 to 3 drops lime juice

2 tbsp. fish sauce

2 tbsp. lime juice

1 tbsp. sugar

2 to 3 tomatoes

1 celery rib

1/2 cucumber

1 each, yellow and red bell pepper, ends trimmed, seeded

2 shallots

3 to 5 spring onions or scallions

2 garlic cloves

2 to 3 fresh large red and/or yellow chilies

1 tbsp. sesame seeds

1 tbsp. chili paste

1 tsp. roasted dried chili flakes

4 red bell peppers, tops cut off, seeds and membranes removed

peppermint leaves, for garnish

SALADS

GLASS NOODLE SALAD

Yum Woon Sen

Soak glass noodles in cold water for 10 minutes, then place in colander and dip briefly into enough boiling water to cover. Remove colander and place noodles under cold running water. Drain well.

Cut chicken breast into small pieces and sauté in a non-stick skillet with a touch of lime juice and water. Combine fish sauce, lime juice and sugar and heat briefly until sugar dissolves. Set aside to cool.

Cut cucumber, pepper and shallots into bite-sized pieces. Cut white portion of spring onions into 1–inch pieces and slice green stalks into thin rolls. Set aside green rolls for garnish. Mix noodles together with cut vegetables, mushrooms, dried prawns, peanuts, peppermint leaves and chicken. Toss well.

To serve, sprinkle cooled sauce over salad and garnish with minced chilies and reserved spring onion rolls.

• • • • • • • • • • • • • •

3 oz. glass noodles

6 oz. chicken breast

2 to 3 drops lime juice

1/2 tsp. water

2 tbsp. fish sauce

2 tbsp. lime juice

1 tbsp. sugar

1/2 cucumber

1 red bell pepper, ends trimmed
  and seeded

2 shallots

4 spring onions or scallions

2 tbsp. Chinese dried mushrooms,
  soaked for 1–2 hours in cold
  water

1 tbsp. dried prawns

1 tbsp. fresh unsalted peanuts

peppermint leaves, to taste

fresh chilies, to taste

SALADS

Papaya & Prawn Salad

Som Tam Goong

Peel papaya and cut flesh into very thin strips. Quarter tomatoes. Crush garlic, chilies and peanuts in a mortar or garlic press. Cut beans into 1–inch pieces and crush lightly in mortar. In a large bowl, combine papaya, crushed ingredients and beans together with tomatoes and dried shrimp. Arrange salad mixture onto lettuce leaves.

Combine fish sauce, lime juice and sugar and heat briefly until sugar dissolves. Set aside to cool.

Shell prawns, halve lengthwise and devein. Coat prawns with fish sauce, dust with flour and fry in vegetable oil until golden. Drain on paper towels.

To serve, spoon cooled sauce over salad arrangement and top with prawns.

• • • • • • • • • • • • • •

1 green papaya

2 tomatoes

2 garlic cloves

2 to 3 red and/or green chilies

2 tbsp. fresh unsalted peanuts

4 to 5 yard-long beans

3 tbsp. small dried shrimp

fresh leaf lettuce

2 tbsp. fish sauce

2 tbsp. lime juice

1 tbsp. sugar

4 to 8 prawns

fish sauce, to taste

flour

vegetable oil

S A L A D S

SLICED BEEF SALAD

Yum Neua

Dice or slice vegetables. Slice beef into thin strips and sear in an ungreased, non-stick skillet over very high heat. Set aside to cool, then mix in vegetables.

Combine fish sauce, lime juice, sugar and some chili flakes and heat until sugar dissolves. Set side until cool.

To serve, arrange beef and vegetables in a serving bowl or platter. Drizzle with cooled sauce and garnish with peppermint leaves.

● ● ● ● ● ● ● ● ● ● ● ● ● ●

1 to 2 shallots
4 to 5 spring onions or scallions
1 each, red and green pepper, ends trimmed, seeded
1/2 cucumber,
12 oz. beef filet
2 tbsp. fish sauce
2 tbsp. lime juice
1 tbsp. sugar
coarsely ground chili flakes, to taste
peppermint leaves, for garnish

SAUTÉED PORK SALAD

Yum Moo Nahm Tok

Sauté pork in hot oil until cooked through, yet tender. Carefully transfer to a cutting board and cut into bite-sized pieces. Sauté rice until in an ungreased skillet over low heat until golden brown, then crush in a mortar along with dried chilies. Mince shallots and finely chop spring onions.

Combine pork with shallots and chilies in a mixing bowl. Season with lime juice and fish sauce. Mix in onions and peppermint leaves. Serve immediately, accompanied by seasonal greens.

● ● ● ● ● ● ● ● ● ● ● ● ● ●

1 1/3 lbs. lean pork (whole)
2 tbsp. peanut oil
2 tbsp. uncooked rice
2 to 3 large dried chilies
1 to 2 shallots
4 to 6 spring onions or scallions
2 tbsp. lime juice
1 tbsp. fish sauce
peppermint leaves, for garnish
fresh seasonal greens

SALADS

Egg Noodle Salad with Pork-Stuffed Broccoli Leaves

Ba Mee Jok Kwahn Dong

Brown pork in oil until cooked through. Season with pepper and fish sauce and set aside. Mince garlic and fry until golden brown. Set aside.

Finely chop spring onions. Cut chilies into strips, place in vinegar and allow to marinate during remaining recipe preparation.

Boil egg noodles according to directions, then plunge into cold water. Drain. Blanch broccoli leaves in boiling water, then cool in ice water. Drain.

To prepare, spread out a layer of broccoli leaves. On top of each leaf, place a layer of noodles, followed by a layer of cooked pork and a sprinkle of fried garlic. Top with cilantro leaves, then roll up each leaf, using leaf stem to secure. Serve rolls whole or cut up and garnished with finely chopped spring onions. Arrange marinated chilies on the side.

• 50 •

● ● ● ● ● ● ● ● ● ● ● ● ● ●

12 oz. minced pork
2 tbsp. peanut oil
freshly-ground pepper, to taste
fish sauce, to taste
2 to 3 garlic cloves
3 to 5 spring onions or scallions
2 to 3 fresh large chilies
1/3 cup white vinegar
6 oz. fresh egg noodles
5 to 6 Chinese broccoli leaves
cilantro leaves, to taste

LARGE MIXED SALAD

Yum Yai

Cut cucumber, tomatoes, lettuce and spring onions into bite-sized pieces. Toast peanuts in an oven or skillet, without oil, then finely chop. Remove leaves from celery, cilantro and peppermint and set aside. Finely slice celery ribs and chop cilantro stems and roots. Slice chilies and carrot into thin strips. Slice shallots and marinated garlic cloves.

Soak glass noodles in cold water for 10 minutes, then place in colander and dip briefly into enough boiling water to cover. Remove and place noodles under cold running water. Drain well, then coarsly chop.

Stir together lime juice, soy sauce, reserved garlic marinade, salt and sugar, adjusting quantities as required to achieve desired flavor balance.

In a serving bowl, mix together salad ingredients and noodles. Add sauce and toss well.

● ● ● ● ● ● ● ● ● ● ● ● ● ●

1 cucumber

2 to 3 tomatoes

1 to 2 heads of iceberg lettuce

2 to 4 spring onions or scallions

4 oz. fresh unsalted peanuts

2 to 3 celery ribs

1 bunch of cilantro (with roots)

1 bunch peppermint

2 to 4 fresh large red chilies

1 carrot

2 shallots

4 to 6 marinated garlic cloves, plus
   1 tbsp. reserved marinade

1 package of glass noodles

juice of 2 limes

2 to 3 tbsp. light soy sauce

salt, to taste

sugar, to taste

SOUPS

1n the symphony that is Thai cooking, soup, or *tom,* is the allegro; a stridently paced whirlwind of ingredients, enraptured with fragrance. The incomparable taste of Thai soups stems from lemon grass, lime leaves, galangal, lemon or lime juice and, of course, *nahm pla,* the spicy fish sauce. Most soups are based on the same type of stock (whether beef, chicken or fish), which is usually prepared and stored conveniently and therefore always on hand to create a small delicacy. Soups are named after the different herbs and spices added to stock, the combinations of which provide for incomparable taste variations. *Tom* can range from being devilishly spicy by the addition of chilies, to being milder, velvety and smooth, thanks to coconut milk.

Tom is a very much-loved part of the Thailand cuisine. Like rice, steaming soup is a main part of the Thai table setting and remains there throughout the meal, always ready to be tasted to rekindle appetites, to titillate the palate and to calm the tummy. Unlike Western practice, *tom* is not considered strictly an introductory course. It plays many roles—as appetizer, main course, or last course. The eating of soup is also not limited to time of day. Thais love *tom* any time of the day—for breakfast, lunch, snacks and, of course, dinner. For them, it is difficult to conceive of a meal without it. A ginger soup with chicken and rice, for example can be part of a Thai breakfast right along with coffee or tea and fruit.

For Thais, no other food boosts the spirit like *tom.* The most royal of all soups, T*om Yum Goong* (page 54), will convince even the most unbending skeptic of this. The freshness and balanced spiciness of the stock enriched with prawns—and in our recipe, with oyster mushrooms—along with fresh herbs will provide a unique taste experience.

Prawn Soup with Lemon Grass

Tom Yum Goong

Trim off and discard tips of galangal root and then pound with a kitchen mallet until full aroma is released. Pound lemon grass. Crush lime leaves by hand. Add these spices to stock and simmer for 1 to 2 hours. Strain stock.

Shell prawns, halve lengthwise, devein and cut into bite-sized pieces. Chop mushrooms and tomatoes and, together with prawns, add to stock. Bring to a low boil. Season with desired balance of fish sauce, lime juice and chili paste.

Just before serving, return soup to a boil and sprinkle with a few drops of chili oil. Garnish with thinly-sliced spring onions and cilantro leaves. If desired, add dried chilies for decoration.

• • • • • • • • • • • • •

1/2 galangal root

1 to 2 stalks lemon grass

4 to 6 fresh Kaffir lime leaves

2 cups stock

4 prawns

2 to 3 oyster mushrooms

4 tomatoes

fish sauce, to taste

lime juice, to taste

1 to 2 tbsp. chili paste

chili oil

2 to 3 spring onions or scallions

1/2 bunch cilantro leaves

dried chilies, for garnish

SOUPS

GLASS NOODLE SOUP WITH CHICKEN
Tom Gaeng Chud Woon Sen

Mince garlic and fry in oil until golden brown. Set aside. Soak glass noodles in cold water for 10 minutes, then place in colander and dip briefly into enough boiling water to cover. Remove and place under cold running water. Drain well and set aside.

Finely chop chicken breast, sprinkle with soy sauce and fish sauce and mix well. Shape balls from chicken mixture. Cut white portion of spring onions into 1–inch pieces and slice green stalks into thin rolls. Reserve green rolls for garnish. Finely chop shallot.

Add chicken balls, white spring onion pieces, mushrooms and shallot to stock. Bring to a boil and balance and season with desired balance of fish sauce, light soy sauce and sugar. Continue cooking until chicken becomes tender.

To serve, transfer glass noodles into soup bowls, then sprinkle with fried garlic and a little white pepper. Spoon soup over dish and garnish with reserved spring onion rolls.

Note: This soup can be prepared with tofu chunks instead of chicken.

• • • • • • • • • • • • • •
- 2 to 3 garlic cloves
- 1 tbs. peanut oil
- 1 handful of glass noodles
- 4 oz. boneless, skinless chicken breast
- light soy sauce, to taste
- fish sauce, to taste
- 4 to 6 spring onions or scallions
- 1 shallot
- 2 cups stock
- 2 tbsp. Chinese dried mushrooms, soaked for 1–2 hours in cold water
- sugar, to taste
- freshly-ground white pepper, to taste

SOUPS

CHICKEN & COCONUT SOUP

Tom Kha Gai

Combine coconut milk and stock in a pot. Cut and discard tips of galangal root, then pound root with a kitchen mallet to release aroma. Coarsely chop lemon grass and pound. Crush lime leaves by hand. Add galangal root, lemon grass and lime leaves to coconut milk and stock and simmer over low heat for 1 to 2 hours. Strain.

Cut chicken breast and shallots into small pieces, add to stock mixture and bring to a boil. Season with desired balance of fish sauce, lime juice and sugar.

Before serving, sprinkle soup with a few drops of chili oil and garnish with cilantro leaves and thinly-sliced spring onion.

Note: For a spicier soup, you may add dried or ground chilies.

• 58 •

● ● ● ● ● ● ● ● ● ● ● ● ●

2 cups coconut milk

2 cups stock

1 small galangal root

2 sprigs of lemon grass

4 fresh Kaffir lime leaves

6 oz. boneless, skinless chicken breast

1 to 2 shallots or spring onions

fish sauce, to taste

lime juice, to taste

sugar, to taste

chili oil, to taste

cilantro leaves, for garnish

1 spring onion or scallion

SOUPS

EGG NOODLE SOUP WITH PURÉED CHICKEN

Tom Mee Sah

Cut noodles into 3–inch pieces. Purée chicken breast. Pound cilantro roots, peppercorns and half of the garlic cloves in a mortar. Transfer to a small mixing bowl and season spices with soy sauce and fish sauce. Mix in puréed chicken. Mince remaining garlic and fry in oil until golden brown. Set aside for later garnish. Cut spring onions and celery into bite-sized pieces. Heat stock to simmering, add onions and celery, remove from heat, then let stand. Season stock with additional soy sauce and fish sauce.

Form patties approximately 3/4–inch thick out of chicken purée. Top each patty with noodles, making sure noodles extend over edge of meat, then roll up. Return soup to simmering, add meat rolls and cook over low heat for 5 minutes. Check and adjust seasoning.

Before serving, sprinkle soup with reserved fried garlic and finely-chopped cilantro leaves.

Note: Instead of filling the meat rolls with noodles, the noodles may be cooked in advance, then added to soup just before serving.

• • • • • • • • • • • • •

3 oz. fresh egg noodles

6 oz. boneless, skinless chicken breast

2 cilantro roots

1 tbsp. whole peppercorns

6 to 7 garlic cloves

light soy sauce, to taste

fish sauce, to taste

1 tbsp. peanut oil

3 to 4 spring onions or scallions

1 celery rib

4 cups stock

1/2 bunch of cilantro leaves

COCONUT SOUP WITH MUSSELS

Tom Kha Hoy Lay

Scrub and debeard mussels. Heat coconut milk and stock in a pot. Cut galangal root and lemon grass small pieces. Pound pieces with kitchen mallet to release aroma, then add to coconut milk and stock. Simmer for 1 hour.

Thinly slice shallots and garlic and add to stock. Thinly slice half of the spring onions and set aside for later garnish. Cut remaining half of onions along with all the chilies into small pieces and add to stock. Season with desired balance of fish sauce and lime juice.

Shortly before serving, add mussels and heat through until they open. Garnish with reserved spring onions and serve immediately.

● ● ● ● ● ● ● ● ● ● ● ● ● ●

1 lb. fresh mussels or clams
2 cups coconut milk
2 cups stock
1/2 galangal root
1 stalk lemon grass
1 to 2 shallots
2 garlic cloves
4 to 6 spring onions or scallions
2 to 3 large fresh chilies
fish sauce, to taste
lime juice, to taste

SOUPS

RICE & GINGER SOUP
Khao Tom Gai King

ince two to three of the garlic cloves and sauté until in 1 tablespoon oil until golden brown. Thinly slice spring onions. Pick leaves off cilantro stems. Set aside garlic, spring onions and cilantro leaves for later garnish.

Crush cilantro root with the remaining garlic cloves in a mortar. Separately crush dried chili flakes. Slice celery and fresh chilies. Peel and slice ginger root, then cut slices into very thin strips. Cut chicken breast into bite-sized pieces.

Heat remaining 2 tablespoons oil in wok and stir-fry cilantro-garlic mixture, dried chili flakes, celery, fresh chilies, and ginger. Season with pepper. Add stock and heat to a fast simmer. Add chicken and cook until tender. Season with desired balance of fish sauce, soy sauce and pepper.

Before serving, add cooked rice and bring to a brief boil. Garnish with reserved cilantro leaves, garlic and onions. Serve immediately.

• • • • • • • • • • • • • •

5 to 7 garlic cloves

3 tbsp. peanut oil

4 to 5 spring onions or scallions

1 bunch cilantro (with root)

1 tsp. dried chili flakes

1 rib celery

2 large fresh chilies

1 young ginger root

1 lb. boneless, skinless chicken breast

freshly ground pepper

1 quart stock

fish sauce, to taste

light soy sauce, to taste

2 cups cooked rice

SOUPS

COCONUT SOUP WITH PRAWNS & POTATOES

Tom Kha Man Farang Goong

Combine coconut milk and stock in a pot. Chop galangal and lemon grass into small pieces, then pound with a kitchen mallet until full aroma is released. Crush lime leaves by hand. Add galangal, lemon grass and lime leaves to stock and simmer for 1 hour. Strain. Peel and dice potatoes and add to soup. While soup is simmering, shell prawns, halve lengthwise, devein and cut into bite-sized pieces. Set aside.

When potatoes are cooked, season soup with desired balance of fish sauce, lime juice and finely-chopped chilies. Just before serving, add prawns and bring to a brief boil. Garnish with cilantro leaves and a few drops of chili oil.

• • • • • • • • • • • • •

2 cups coconut milk

2 cups stock

1/2 galangal root

1 stalk lemon grass

4 fresh Kaffir lime leaves

4 potatoes

4 to 8 prawns

fish sauce, to taste

lime juice, to taste

fresh chilies, to taste

1 bunch cilantro leaves

chili oil, to taste

LEMON GRASS SOUP WITH VEGETABLES

Tom Yum Mangsawirat

Trim off and discard tips of galangal root. Coarsely chop root and lemon grass, then pound with a kitchen mallet until full aroma is released. Crush lime leaves by hand. Bring stock to a simmer, then add galangal, lemon grass and lime leaves. Simmer for 1 hour, then strain. Cut vegetables and tofu into bite-sized pieces, add to soup and cook until soft. Season with desired balance of soy sauce, fish sauce and lime juice. Before serving, add cilantro leaves, and, if desired, minced chilies and a few drops of chili oil.

• • • • • • • • • • • • •

1 galangal root

1 stalk lemon grass

6 lime leaves

4 cups stock

4 oyster mushrooms

4 to 6 ears baby corn

1 rib of celery

1 1/3 lbs. Chinese watercress

3 oz. tofu

light soy sauce, to taste

fish sauce and lime juice, to taste

1 bunch cilantro leaves

fresh large chilies (optional)

chili oil (optional)

Tom Yum Mangsawirat

SOUPS

GINGER SOUP WITH RED SNAPPER

Tom Yum Khamin Pla Soth

Coarsely chop lemon grass and pound with a kitchen mallet until full aroma is released. Crush lime leaves by hand. Heat stock to a low boil, add lemon grass and lime leaves and simmer for 1 hour. Strain stock.

Slice fish filets into portions. Halve tomatoes, coarsely chop shallots and thinly slice garlic. Peel and slice ginger root, then cut slices into very thin strips.

Add tomatoes, shallots, garlic and ginger to strained stock and bring to a low boil. Season with desired balance of fish sauce, lime juice and minced chilies, Add fish pieces to soup and cook at a simmer until fish is cooked through. Garnish with cilantro leaves and thinly-sliced spring onions.

● ● ● ● ● ● ● ● ● ● ● ● ●

1 stalk lemon grass

6 fresh Kaffir lime leaves

4 cups stock

1 3/4 lbs. red snapper, grey mullet, or other saltwater fish

6 to 8 cherry tomatoes

1 to 2 shallots

2 to 3 garlic cloves

1 young ginger root

fish sauce, to taste

lime juice, to taste

small fresh chilies, to taste

1/2 bunch cilantro leaves

4 to 6 spring onions or scallions

SOUPS

CURRIES

Thailand's curry dishes are the furioso in the symphony of Thai cooking—blazing, stormy, a never-ending obsession. Fiery to those not accustomed to Thai cooking, their intense pungency puts beads of perspiration on foreheads, stuns the senses, yet leaves one eager for the next taste sensation.

Thai curries, or even curry pastes for that matter, are not to be confused with the well-known yellow spice. Curry pastes—truly an expression of artistry in taste, diversity and harmony—form the basis of the dishes also designated as "curries." Unlike Western cooking, meat is not seared before basting, but is instead added raw to the curry paste which is then diluted with coconut milk or soup stock. Preferably, only tender fish and seafood meats are mixed into the curry just before serving.

Thai cooking relies on four basic curry pastes: red, green, Massaman and Panaeng (Recipes are found on pages 127–130). Red curry paste, made from red chili pods, is well suited for use with all meats. Fresh green pods make the difference in green pastes which go well with white meats (chicken and veal) as well as with fish. Massaman curry is usually prepared with potatoes and apples, and, although less hot than other curry pastes, its spicy and sweet-sour taste combination makes it suitable for use with fish and in most other dishes. Panaeng curry paste offers an extraordinary taste experience, the result of a perfect balance of flavors accented by peanuts, the salt in fish sauce and the intense intonation of lime leaves. Panaeng curry can be used with all meats, fish and seafood.

Curry pastes (as well as chili pastes) can be prepared in advance and kept either in the refrigerator for up to a week or frozen in portions. However, if time is short and no homemade paste is on hand, fresh, imported, quality pastes may be obtained from Western specialty stores.

GREEN CURRY WITH BEEF

Gaeng Kiew Wan Neua

Cut beef into bite-sized pieces. Sauté curry paste in oil, then slowly stir in coconut milk. Add stock and beef and bring to a simmer. Meanwhile, cut chilies into thin rings and beans into 1–inch pieces. Quarter or slice eggplants, depending on size. Add chilies, beans and eggplant to curry mixture and return to a simmer. Season with desired balance of fish sauce and sugar. Roll up lime leaves and slice into thin strips. Add leaves to curry and continue simmering. If necessary, add stock to thin. Sprinkle with basil leaves before serving.

Note: This curry can be prepared with beef, chicken or prawns. Remember that meat is added to curry raw, then cooked until tender.

● ● ● ● ● ● ● ● ● ● ● ●
1 1/2 lbs. beef filet
1 tbsp. green curry paste
2 tbsp. peanut oil
2/3 cup coconut milk
2 cups stock
3 to 4 large red and yellow chilies
5 to 6 yard-long beans
4 to 6 Thai eggplants
fish sauce, to taste
sugar, to taste
3 to 4 fresh Kaffir lime leaves
Thai basil leaves, for garnish

GREEN CURRY WITH FRESH COCONUT

Maprao Ohn Song Kruang

This curry uses the same ingredients as in the recipe above but incorporates fresh, instead of canned, coconut milk. To prepare, hollow out coconut, cut meat into strips and combine with vegetables.

The finished curry is then served in a lightly-warmed coconut shell and served immediately.

Gaeng Kiew Wan Neua

CURRIES

MASSAMAN CURRY WITH CHICKEN

Massaman Gai

Sauté curry paste peanut oil until full aroma is released. Slowly add coconut milk, stirring well. Stir in stock. Season with desired balance of fish sauce, lime juice and sugar.

Cut chicken into bite-sized pieces. Peel and dice potatoes and apples and mince shallot. Combine potatoes and apples with chicken, shallot and peanuts and add to curry. Simmer until chicken and potatoes are cooked. If necessary, correct seasoning and add additional stock to thin curry.

Note: This curry can also be prepared using pork or beef. Remember that meat is added to curry raw, then cooked until tender.

• • • • • • • • • • • • • •

1 tbsp. massaman curry paste

1 tbsp. peanut oil

$2/3$ cup coconut milk

2 cups stock

fish sauce, to taste

lime juice, to taste

sugar, to taste

$1^1/2$ lbs. boneless, skinless chicken breast

5 medium-sized potatoes

1 each, red and green apple

1 shallot

2 tbsp. fresh unsalted peanuts

RED CURRY WITH STEAMED CHICKEN

Gai Pim

Purée chicken breast. Cut spring onions into small pieces. Pick leaves off cilantro stems and set aside. Crush cilantro root in a mortar. Slice chilies. Beat eggs until foamy.

Blend together puréed chicken, curry paste and chilies. Add coconut milk and fold in beaten eggs. Add spring onions and cilantro leaves. Season with desired balance of fish sauce and sugar. Portion mixture into soup bowls or small gratin dishes and steam for approximately 30 minutes or until cooked through.

• • • • • • • • • • • • • •

$1^1/2$ lbs. boneless, skinless chicken breast

4 to 6 spring onions or scallions

1 bunch cilantro

3 to 4 large chilies

4 eggs

1 to 2 tbsp. red curry paste

$3/4$ cup coconut milk

fish sauce, to taste

sugar, to taste

Massaman Gai

CURRIES

RED CURRY WITH CHICKEN

Gaeng Gai Nah Mai

Cut chicken into bite-sized pieces. Slice bamboo shoot into strips. Sauté curry paste in oil until full aroma is released. Slowly add coconut milk to paste, stirring constantly. Add bamboo strips and chicken and continue stirring. Add stock, then season with desired balance of fish sauce and sugar. Cut chili into rings and add. Before serving, bring mixture to a boil and sprinkle with basil leaves.

Note: This curry can also be prepared using pork. Remember that meat is added to curry raw, then cooked until tender.

● ● ● ● ● ● ● ● ● ● ● ● ●

1 1/2 lbs. boneless, skinless chicken breast
1 bamboo shoot (fresh or canned)
1 tbsp. red curry paste
2 tbsp. peanut oil
3/4 cup coconut milk
2 cups stock
fish sauce, to taste
sugar, to taste
1 large fresh chili, to taste
1 bunch Thai basil

RED CURRY WITH CHICKEN & YARD-LONG BEANS

Gai Phat Prik King Tuafang Yiew

Set basil leaves soaking in water. Cut chicken breast and beans into bite-sized pieces. Roll up lime leaves and slice into thin strips. Thinly slice chilies. Sauté curry paste in oil until full aroma is released. Add beans, lime leaves and chicken and brown. Add stock and season with desired balance of fish sauce and sugar. Add chilies.

Before serving, drain basil leaves and mix into curry.

● ● ● ● ● ● ● ● ● ● ● ● ●

Thai basil, to taste
1 1/2 lbs. boneless, skinless chicken breast
5 to 6 yard-long beans
2 to 3 fresh Kaffir lime leaves
3 to 4 large chilies
1 to 2 tbsp. red curry paste
2 tbsp. peanut oil
1/2 cup stock
fish sauce, to taste
sugar, to taste

Gaeng Gai Nah Mai

CURRIES

Red Curry with Beef & Krachai Root

Neua Phat Prik Bai Krachai

Cut beef into bite-sized pieces. Trim off and discard tips of krachai root, then thinly slice. Cut beans into bite-sized pieces and slice chilies on the diagonal into rings. Roll up lime leaves and slice into thin strips.

Sauté curry paste in oil until full aroma is released, then add krachai roots, beans, chilies, lime leaves, and green pepper and brown. Add stock, then beef. Return to a simmer and cook until tender. Season with desired balance of fish sauce and sugar. Sprinkle with basil leaves before serving.

• 76 •

• • • • • • • • • • • • •

1 1/2 lbs. beef filet

6 to 8 krachai roots

2 to 3 yard-long beans

3 to 4 large chilies

2 to 3 fresh Kaffir lime leaves

1 to 2 tbsp. red curry paste

2 tbsp. peanut oil

1 to 2 tbsp. chopped green pepper

3/4 cup stock

fish sauce, to taste

sugar, to taste

Thai basil leaves, for garnish

CURRIES

PANAENG CURRY WITH PRAWNS
Goong Panaeng

Roll up lime leaves and slice into thin strips. Finely chop peanuts. Cut spring onions into 1-inch pieces and thinly slice shallots. Slice chilies into thin rings.

In a wok or deep skillet, sauté curry paste in oil until full aroma is released. Gradually add coconut milk and stock, stirring constantly. Add lime leaves, peanuts, onions and shallots and bring to a low boil. If necessary, thin mixture with additional stock. Season with desired balance of fish sauce and sugar. Add chilies and sprinkle with basil leaves.

While curry is cooking, shell prawns, halve lengthwise and devein. Sauté briefly in hot vegetable oil. Drain on paper towels. Add to curry or serve separately.

Note: This curry can be also prepared with fish, beef, lamb (without fat) and chicken. Remember that meat is added to curry raw, then cooked until tender. Fish and seafood, however, should either be served separately or fried before adding to curry.

• • • • • • • • • • • • •

3 fresh Kaffir lime leaves

1 tbsp. fresh unsalted peanuts

2 to 4 spring onions or scallions

1 to 2 shallots

1 each, large red and yellow chili

1 to 2 tbsp. Panaeng curry paste

2 tbsp. peanut oil

3/4 cup coconut milk

1/2 cup stock

fish sauce, to taste

sugar, to taste

Thai basil leaves, to taste

4 to 8 prawns

vegetable oil

CURRIES

MEAT & POULTRY

While potent curry dishes and their beguiling fiery pungency sharply heighten the senses, meat and fish courses chart the Thai meal into calmer waters and gently caress the senses, pampering the palate with a host of taste nuances: sweet, sour, spicy, or mild. They are the andante movement in the Thai symphony of culinary delights.

Beef, *neua,* and chicken, *gai,* occupy center stage. Beef works wonderfully well with individual or combined vegetables, nuts, roots, or noodles. As in all Thai cooking the spiciness of meat is derived from chilies, with a mild counterbalance of sweet, creamy coconut milk or sugar. Chicken, always available and reasonably priced throughout Thailand, enjoys a greater popularity than higher-priced beef. Chicken dishes also provide the most variety in Thai cooking. In our recipes poultry is often wrapped in leaves, stuffed inside tomatoes, or combined with rice and vegetables. Subtle in taste, *gai* enhances the palette of tastes in Thai cooking. It can even be combined with fish as in our splendid *Pla Hao Mok* (page 108). In Thai cooking, all meats are always cut into bite-sized pieces and therefore require only a short cooking time, most often in a sauce or with vegetables.

Tourists visiting Thailand's cities and beaches are not often exposed the country's agricultural heartland and the vital role it plays in Thai cuisine. Thailand's granary has always been the expansive fertile lowland in the heart of the country where most of the population resides in rural areas. Like their ancestors, the people live off their fields and harvests and it is from here that theindispensable meats, fruits, vegetables and grains come that provide the glorious tastes found in Thai cooking.

SAUTÉED BEEF WITH KRACHAI ROOT

Neua Phat Krachai

● ● ● ● ● ● ● ● ● ● ● ● ●

Cut beef into bite-sized pieces and set aside. Trim off and discard tips of krachai root and finely slice. Set aside.

Roll up lime leaves and slice into thin strips. Mince shallots and finely chop one of the chilies. Crush lime leaves, shallots, chopped chilies and shrimp paste in a mortar, mixing together well. In a deep skillet or wok, sauté this paste in hot oil until full aroma is released. Add beef.

When beef is well browned, slowly add coconut milk, stirring constantly. Season with fish sauce. Slice remaining chilies into thin rings. Add chilies, basil leaves and krachai root to curry. Bring to a brief boil, then serve immediately.

If desired, serve curry surrounded by a ring of rice.

1 1/2 lbs. beef filet
6 to 8 krachai roots
2 to 3 fresh Kaffir lime leaves
1 to 2 shallots
2 to 3 large chilies
1/2 tsp. shrimp paste
2 tbsp. peanut oil
3/4 cup coconut milk
fish sauce, to taste
Thai basil leaves, to taste
2 cups cooked rice (optional)

MEAT & POULTRY

Beef with Fried Rice Noodles & Chinese Broccoli

Phat Siya Neua

Soak rice noodles in cold water until soft, then drain well. Cut beef into bite-sized pieces. Peel broccoli stems and cut into flat strips. Coarsely chop broccoli leaves. Chop peanuts.

Heat oil in wok or deep skillet and add broccoli stems and leaves. Add beef and brown well. Add noodles, then quickly stir in eggs. Season with desired balance of fish sauce and light soy sauce and a dash of dark soy sauce. Add sugar and chili powder to taste. Add peanuts. If consistency of dish is too thick, add a small amount of stock to thin.

If desired, sprinkle with fried garlic before serving.

• • • • • • • • • • • • •

1 package wide rice noodles

1 1/3 lbs. beef filet

4 stems of Chinese broccoli

1 tbsp. fresh unsalted peanuts

2 tbsp. peanut oil

2 eggs, beaten

fish sauce, to taste

light soy sauce, to taste

dark soy sauce, to taste

2 tsp. sugar

chili powder, to taste

stock, if necessary

fried minced garlic (optional)

MEAT & POULTRY

Beef with Egg Noodles & Vegetables

Ba Mee Laht Nah Neua

Soak noodles in lukewarm water until soft, then drain well. Cut beef into bite-sized pieces. Rinse soy bean seeds thoroughly. Cut red pepper into strips. Peel broccoli stems and slice both broccoli stems and leaves on the diagonal. Mince garlic and fry in oil. Set garlic aside.

In lightly-oiled wok, brown broccoli pieces, baby corn and pepper first, then add beef. Add soybean seeds and season with desired balance of oyster sauce, soy sauce and fish sauce. Add sugar and stir in stock. For a spicier taste, add peppercorns. Simmer until beef is done. Stir in tapioca flour to thicken to desired consistency.

Cook egg noodles in boiling water, transfer to a colander and place under cold, running water. Drain well. Transfer noodles to a serving platter and mix in fried garlic. Arrange beef and vegetables around noodles and serve.

• • • • • • • • • • • • • • •

8 oz. very fine egg noodles

1 1/3 lbs. beef filet

1 tbsp. soybean seeds

1 red bell pepper, ends trimmed, seeded

3 to 4 stems Chinese broccoli

2 to 3 garlic cloves

1 tbsp. peanut oil

4 to 6 ears baby corn

oyster sauce, to taste

light soy sauce, to taste

fish sauce, to taste

1/4 tsp. sugar

2 cups stock

whole peppercorns (optional)

tapioca flour, for thickening

MEAT & POULTRY

Stir-Fried Beef with Cashews

Neua Phat Met Mamuang

Cut beef into strips. Chop peppers and spring onions and set aside. Finely chop shallots and garlic and fry in 1 tablespoon oil until golden brown.

In a wok or deep skillet, brown beef pieces together with cashew nuts in 2 tablespoons oil. Add mushrooms, shallots, garlic, peppers and continue to brown. Season with desired balance of oyster sauce, soy sauce and fish sauce. Add spring onions and stir in enough stock to arrive at desired consistency. Cook until beef is done, adjusting seasoning, if necessary.

● ● ● ● ● ● ● ● ● ● ● ●

1 1/2 lbs. beef filet
2 bell peppers, red and/or yellow, ends trimmed, seeded
6 spring onions or scallions
2 to 3 shallots
3 to 4 garlic cloves
3 tbsp. peanut oil
4 to 5 tbsp. cashew nuts
2 tbsp. Chinese dried mushrooms, soaked for 1–2 hours in cold water, then drained
1 tbsp. oyster sauce, to taste
1 tbsp. light soy sauce, to taste
fish sauce, to taste
1/4 to 3/4 cup stock

MEAT & POULTRY

EGGPLANT STUFFED WITH RED BEEF CURRY
Gaeng Phat Neua Yud Sai Ma Kua

Finely grind beef. Halve eggplants lengthwise and fry each half in oil until pulp is cooked through. Drain on paper towels and, when slightly cooled, scoop out and chop eggplant pulp. Set hollowed halves aside for later filling.

In a wok or deep skillet, heat coconut milk and gradually stir in curry paste. Bring to a simmer and when full aroma is released, add beef and cook until tender. Season with desired balance of fish sauce and sugar. Mix in chopped eggplant and basil leaves. Fill hollow eggplant halves with mixture and heat briefly in oven. Serve immediately.

● ● ● ● ● ● ● ● ● ● ● ●

1 1/3 lbs. beef filet
4 to 6 Thai eggplants
1 to 2 tbsp. peanut oil
2/3 cup coconut milk
1 to 2 tbsp. red curry paste
fish sauce, to taste
sugar, to taste
1 bunch Thai basil leaves

MEAT & POULTRY

CHICKEN WITH SATOW BEANS

Gai Satow

Cut chicken into bite-sized pieces and coat with fish sauce. Remove satow beans from pods, rinse well and cut in half. In a mortar, crush garlic cloves together with cilantro roots. Mince chilies. Set basil leaves soaking in water.

Brown satow beans and chicken pieces in a lightly oiled wok. Add garlic-cilantro mixture and chilies and continue to brown. Add stock. Season with desired balance of fish sauce, light soy sauce and sugar.

To serve, drain basil leaves and mix with beans. Top with chicken mixture.

● ● ● ● ● ● ● ● ● ● ● ●

1 3/4 lbs. boneless, skinless
   chicken breast
fish sauce, to taste
4 to 5 satow bean pods
3 to 4 garlic cloves
2 to 3 cilantro roots
3 to 4 large chilies
1 bunch Thai basil
peanut oil
1/3 cup stock
light soy sauce, to taste
sugar, to taste

FRIED CHICKEN-CORN PATTIES

Gai Thod Khao Phod

Finely chop or grind chicken breast. Purée corn kernels. In a mortar or garlic press, crush cilantro roots together with garlic cloves and peppercorns. Mince shallots. Toss together above ingredients. Add enough beaten egg to bind ingredients well, then season with desired balance of soy sauce and fish sauce.

Form patties approximately 1/2–inch thick from chicken mixture. Lightly flour and fry in hot vegetable oil until golden brown. Serve with salad greens, finely sliced spring onions and a garnish of cilantro leaves.

● ● ● ● ● ● ● ● ● ● ● ●

1 1/3 lbs. boneless, skinless
   chicken breast
1 1/3 lbs. corn kernels
2 to 3 cilantro roots
3 to 4 garlic cloves
1 to 2 tbsp. peppercorns
2 to 3 shallots
2 to 3 eggs, beaten
light soy sauce, to taste
fish sauce, to taste
white flour
vegetable oil, for frying
fresh salad greens
6 to 8 spring onions or scallions
1 bunch cilantro leaves

Gai Satow

MEAT & POULTRY

Stir-Fried Chicken with Chilies & Basil
Gai Phat Prik Bai Krapao

Mince half of the garlic cloves and sauté in 1 tablespoon oil until golden brown. Remove garlic from pan. Sauté half of the basil leaves in existing oil, then remove and drain well. Set aside garlic and basil for later garnish.

Thinly slice remaining garlic cloves and mince shallots. Cut carrots and beans into strips and slice chilies on the diagonal into rings. Cut chicken breast into bite-sized pieces.

In a wok or deep skillet, stir-fry garlic slices, shallots, carrots, beans and chilies in 2 tablespoons hot oil. Add chicken and brown. Season with desired balance of fish sauce, light and dark soy sauces and sugar. Stir in enough stock to achieve desired consistency.

Just before serving, toss in remaining fresh basil leaves. Garnish with reserved fried garlic and basil.

• 94 •

• • • • • • • • • • • • • • •

2 to 3 garlic cloves
3 tbsp. peanut oil
1 bunch Thai basil leaves
1 to 2 shallots
2 carrots
4 to 5 yard-long beans
3 to 4 large chilies
1 1/2 lbs. boneless, skinless
   chicken breast
fish sauce, to taste
light soy sauce, to taste
dark soy sauce, to taste
sugar, to taste
1/4 to 3/4 cup stock

MEAT & POULTRY

MARINATED CHICKEN IN PANDAN LEAVES
Gai Phat Hoy Bai Toy

Soak pandan leaves in cold water for approximately 15 minutes, or until soft enough to bind. Cut chicken breast into 16 pieces. In a mortar, crush cilantro roots together with garlic cloves and peppercorns. Mix crushed spices together in a pot with brandy, light soy sauce, sugar and oil. Marinate chicken pieces in this mixture for 3 hours, turning occasionally.

Remove chicken from marinade, roll in pandan leaves and refrigerate for 1 hour. In a wok or deep skillet, fry wrapped chicken in hot vegetable oil over low heat until chicken is cooked and golden brown.

To prepare sauce, combine remaining ingredients in a pot, adjusting quantities to personal taste, and cook at a boil for 1 to 2 minutes. Cool sauce before serving with chicken.

● ● ● ● ● ● ● ● ● ● ● ● ● ●

16 pandan leaves
1 3/4 lbs. boneless, skinless
  chicken breast
3 to 4 cilantro roots
3 to 4 garlic cloves
1 to 2 tbsp. peppercorns
1 to 2 tbsp. brandy
2 tbsp. light soy sauce
1 tbsp. sugar
1 tbsp. peanut oil
2 tbsp. vegetable oil

● ● ● ● ● ● ● ● ● ● ● ● ● ●

SAUCE:
1/3 cup dark soy sauce
1 to 2 tsp. finely chopped chili
1 to 2 tbsp. light vinegar
1 tsp. sugar
1 to 2 tsp. sesame seeds

MEAT & POULTRY

CHICKEN IN FRIED RICE WITH YARD-LONG BEANS & BASIL

Khao Phat Gai Bai Krapao

Cut chicken into bite-sized pieces. Mince small chili and cut large chili on the diagonal into thin slices. Set sliced large chili aside for later garnish. Cut beans into 1–inch pieces and thinly slice shallots. Coarsely chop garlic. Set basil leaves soaking in water.

In a wok or deep skillet, brown minced chili, beans, shallots and garlic in hot oil. Add chicken pieces and cook until tender. Blend in cooked rice. Season with desired balance of fish sauce, light soy sauce, sugar and pepper. Drain basil leaves well and add.

Cook eggs into a thin omelet. When cool enough to handle, roll up and thinly slice.

To serve, arrange chicken and rice on a serving platter and garnish with omelet slices and reserved chili slices.

● ● ● ● ● ● ● ● ● ● ● ● ● ●

1 1/3 lbs. boneless, skinless
   chicken breast
1 small chili
1 large chili
3 to 4 yard-long beans
1 to 2 shallots
5 to 6 garlic cloves
1 bunch Thai basil leaves
2 tbsp. vegetable oil
4 to 6 cups cooked rice
fish sauce, to taste
light soy sauce, to taste
sugar, to taste
freshly-ground pepper, to taste
2 eggs, beaten

Stir-Fried Chicken with Chinese Broccoli & Ginger

Gai Phat Phak Khanah King

Slice chilies and cover with light soy sauce to marinate. Cut chicken into bite-sized pieces. In a mortar or garlic press, crush cilantro roots together with garlic and pepper. Transfer spices to a bowl and mix together with chicken pieces. Season with desired balance of fish sauce and soy sauce. Set aside for 15 minutes.

Toast sesame seeds in a skillet without oil until golden brown. Set aside for later garnish. Peel and finely slice ginger root. Remove leaves from broccoli and coarsely chop. Peel and slice broccoli stems.

In a wok or deep skillet, stir-fry ginger root and broccoli stems in oil until brown, then add chicken, stirring frequently. Add broccoli leaves, mix well and continue cooking. Season with additional fish sauce and soy sauce. Cook until chicken is tender. If necessary, add stock to thin. Arrange on platter, top with sesame seeds and serve with marinated chilies.

● ● ● ● ● ● ● ● ● ● ● ● ● ●

2 to 3 large chilies
light soy sauce
1 1/2 lbs. boneless, skinless
   chicken breast
2 to 3 cilantro roots
2 to 4 garlic cloves
freshly-ground pepper, to taste
fish sauce, to taste
2 tbsp. sesame seeds
1 young ginger root
4 to 6 stems Chinese broccoli
2 tbps. peanut oil
1/4 cup stock, if necessary

• 99 •

TOMATOES STUFFED WITH CHICKEN
Makeua Teht Daengna Sod Sai

Remove top third of tomatoes. Spoon out pulp and pass through a colander or large-holed sieve. Reserve tomato shells. Purée chicken breast. Mince shallots. In a mortar or garlic press, crush cilantro roots together with garlic and peppercorns.

Combine chicken, tomato pulp, shallots and crushed spices and blend well. Season with desired balance of light soy sauce and fish sauce. Mix well. Spoon mixture into tomato shells and steam for about 20 to 30 minutes. Let cool slightly.

Add a little soy sauce and lime juice to eggs and whisk well. With paper towels, pat dry outside of tomato shells, then dip into beaten egg, making sure to coat well. Using a wok or deep skillet, fry stuffed tomatoes in hot oil.

Cook remaining egg mixture by dipping in a wire whisk and letting egg drip off and into hot oil. When egg is cooked, remove using a slotted spoon.

To serve, garnish tomatoes with cooked egg and serve immediately.

- - - - - - - - - - - - -
4 beefsteak tomatoes
I lb. boneless, skinless chicken breast
2 to 3 shallots
2 to 3 cilantro roots
4 to 6 garlic cloves
I to 2 tbsp. green peppercorns
light soy sauce, to taste
fish sauce, to taste
lime juice, to taste
2 to 3 eggs
peanut oil, for frying

STIR-FRIED CHICKEN WITH BAMBOO, ASPARAGUS & OYSTER MUSHROOMS

Gai Phat Nah Mai Falang

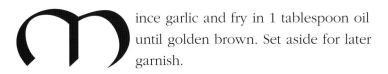

M ince garlic and fry in 1 tablespoon oil until golden brown. Set aside for later garnish.

Cut chicken into bite-sized pieces. Thinly slice carrots. Slice bamboo shoots and mushrooms into strips. Cut white portion of spring onions into 1–inch pieces and slice green stalks into thin rolls. Set rolls aside for later garnish.

In a wok or deep skillet, sauté carrots and bamboo in remaining oil. Add chicken, mushrooms and white spring onion pieces. Brown well. If necessary, add stock to thin. Season with desired balance of pepper, fish sauce, light soy sauce and sugar. Continue cooking until chicken is tender.

Cook asparagus in boiling water until just tender. Drain and serve immediately with chicken. Garnish with reserved spring onions, fried garlic and cilantro leaves.

3 to 4 garlic cloves
2 tbsp. peanut oil
1 1/2 lbs. boneless, skinless
    chicken breast
2 carrots
6 oz. fresh bamboo shoots
3 to 4 oyster mushrooms
4 to 6 spring onions or scallions
stock, if necessary
freshly-ground pepper, to taste
fish sauce, to taste
light soy sauce, to taste
sugar, to taste
1 lb. green asparagus
1 bunch cilantro leaves

DEEP-FRIED CHICKEN TENDERS WITH GINGER SAUCE

Gai Grob Piew Wan

To prepare sauce: peel ginger, cut into thin slices, then cut slices into very thin strips. Sauté in peanut oil until full aroma is released. Stir in lime juice and honey, then add stock. Season with sugar and soy sauce. Thicken mixture by stirring in small amounts of corn meal until desired consistency is achieved.

Cut chicken breast into large bite-sized pieces, marinate in soy sauce for 10 minutes. Remove chicken and coat with corn meal. Transfer to a sieve and shake away excess breading. Dip chicken pieces into beaten eggs. In a wok or deep skillet, deep-fry chicken pieces in hot oil until golden brown. Drain on paper towels.

To serve, garnish with fresh salad greens, finely-sliced spring onions, chilies and sauce on the side.

● ● ● ● ● ● ● ● ● ● ● ● ●

SAUCE:

1 young ginger root

1 tbsp. peanut oil

1 tbsp. lime juice

2 tbsp. honey

3/4 cup stock

1 tbsp. sugar

light soy sauce, to taste

corn meal

● ● ● ● ● ● ● ● ● ● ● ● ●

1 3/4 lbs. boneless, skinless chicken breast

light soy sauce, for marinade

corn meal

4 eggs, beaten

peanut oil, for deep-frying

fresh seasonal salad greens

spring onions, for garnish

chilies, for garnish

MARINATED CHICKEN WINGS

Bik Gai Thod Kratiem Prik Thai

Rinse chicken wings and pat dry with paper towels. In a mortar or garlic press, crush cilantro roots together with garlic and peppercorns. Add soy sauce and sugar. If necessary, mix in a little oil to thin. Place chicken wings in marinade and refrigerate for 2 hours. Remove chicken from marinade and drain. Fry in vegetable oil until golden brown.

● ● ● ● ● ● ● ● ● ● ● ● ●

1 1/2 lbs. chicken wings

4 cilantro roots

6 garlic cloves

1 tbsp. peppercorns

3 tbsp. light soy sauce

1 tbsp. sugar

peanut oil, if necessary

vegetable oil, for frying

Bik Gai Thod Kratiem Prik Thai

MEAT & POULTRY

FISH & SEAFOOD

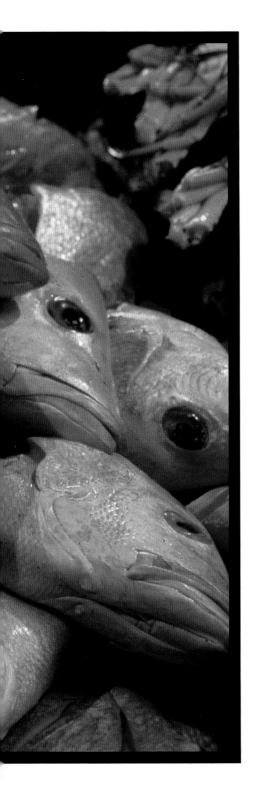

The proximity of the sea can be felt, smelled and tasted throughout Thailand and traces of its bounty pervade all Thai kitchens. Fish, called *pla,* and seafood, *goong,* are part of Thailand's culinary harmony, playing a subdued role in some dishes and taking the spotlight in others. From fish, prawns, crayfish, and crabs, to lobster, mussels, squid and calamari, Thais love all types of seafood. Whether raw, steamed, fried, or grilled, they are a much-loved part of many soups, salads, and main courses.

Thais are true masters in the art of using nature's bounty. Little is thrown away or rejected, especially in cooking with fish and seafood. Fish heads, are just one example. Imaginative Thai cooks find use for whole fishheads in soups or fried as a delicacy and served along with vegetables.

The taste of fish and seafood accentuates even sauces and pastes in Thai cooking. *Nahm pla,* the fish sauce made from fish and prawns fermented in salt, is as indispensable to Thai cooking as soy sauce is to the Chinese or salt to Westerners. Prawn paste also provides sauces, soups and curries with an incomparable tang of the sea. Both of these staple seasonings can be purchased in Asian specialty stores.

Use fresh or uncooked flash-frozen seafood whenever possible and vary recipes in accordance with market availability. Shrimp, crayfish and other shellfish make good substitutions for giant prawns. Also, when preparing boney fish, cut it into small slices or open it on both sides up to the bones, then fry or deep-fry the fish to a crisp. The intense heat crisps the small bones and makes them edible.

OCEAN FISH FILET & GINGER SAUCE

Pla Phat King Soth

Soak soybean seeds and mushrooms into cold water for 1–2 hours. Peel ginger and slice into thin strips. Soak for 1 hour in cold, salted water to remove bitterness. Rinse with clear water before using.

Mince garlic and fry in 1 tablespoon oil until golden brown. Set garlic aside for later garnish. Thinly slice shallots. Dice spring onions and peppers.

Lightly sauté ginger in 1 teaspoon oil. Add shallots, onions and peppers and and stir-fry for a few minutes. Stir in stock, soybeans and mushrooms. Bring mixture to a boil, then season with desired balance of fish sauce, light and dark soy sauces, oyster sauce and sugar. Whisk in enough tapioca flour to achieve desired sauce consistency

Fry filets in hot vegetable oil until golden brown. Drain on paper towels. Arrange fish on a serving platter surrounded by vegetables and sauce. Serve immediately.

• • • • • • • • • • • • •

1 tbsp. soybean seeds
1 tbsp. Chinese dried mushrooms
3 young ginger roots
3 to 4 garlic cloves
1 tbsp. peanut oil
2 shallots
6 to 8 spring onions or scallions
1 each, red and yellow bell
   pepper, ends trimmed, seeded
1 tsp. peanut oil
3/4 stock
fish sauce, to taste
light soy sauce, to taste
dark soy sauce, to taste
oyster sauce, to taste
sugar, to taste
tapioca flour
1 1/3 lbs. ocean fish filets
   (mahi mahi or ocean perch)
vegetable oil

FISH & SEAFOOD

STEAMED FISH WITH CHICKEN & CHINESE CABBAGE

Pla Hao Mok

Cut fish filets into bite-sized pieces. Purée chicken breast. Keep fish and chicken refrigerated until ready to use. Rinse cabbage and cut into fine strips. Blanch cabbage in boiling water and immediately plunge into ice water. Drain and set aside. Roll up lime leaves and slice into thin strips. In a mortar or garlic press, crush together cilantro roots and garlic cloves. Thinly slice chilies.

Combine chicken with curry paste. Mix in eggs, then add just enough coconut milk to bind. Mix in cilantro-garlic mixture, sugar and lime leaves. Season to taste with fish sauce. Place fish filets into this chicken mixture and set aside for 15 minutes.

Layer gratin forms with Chinese cabbage, top with coated fish and sprinkle with sliced chilies. Steam for 15–20 minutes or until fish is cooked through. To serve, drizzle with additional coconut milk and garnish with cilantro leaves.

Note: This dish is traditionally prepared using banana leaves.

• 108 •

• • • • • • • • • • • • • •

$1^{1}/3$ lbs. fish filets (ocean perch, sole, or cod)

3 oz. boneless, skinless chicken breast

1 Chinese cabbage

4 to 6 fresh Kaffir lime leaves

2 to 3 cilantro roots

3 to 4 garlic cloves

3 to 4 large Thai chilies

2 to 3 tbsp. red curry paste

2 eggs, beaten

$3/4$ cup coconut milk

1 tbsp. sugar

fish sauce, to taste

cilantro leaves, for garnish

109 · 109 ·

FISH & SEAFOOD

Fish in Coconut Sauce

Pla Tom Yum Khati

Scale and rinse fish thoroughly. Keep refrigerated until ready to use. Pick cilantro leaves off stems and set aside for later garnish. Coarsely chop lemon grass, then pound with a kitchen mallet, together with cilantro roots and galangal root, until full aroma is released. Crush lime leaves by hand.

Combine coconut milk and stock in a pot large enough to accommodate a whole fish. Heat to a low boil then add lemon grass, cilantro and galangal roots and lime leaves. Reduce heat and simmer for 1 hour. Strain.

Remove large leaves from banana flower and cut inner part into thin slices (halve slices if too large). Finely slice chilies and add to broth, along with banana flower slices. Bring broth back up to a simmer and season with desired balance of fish sauce and lime juice. Add fish and simmer until cooked through. Transfer fish and broth into a deep serving platter and garnish with reserved cilantro leaves.

• • • • • • • • • • • • •

1 3/4 lbs. fresh whole fish
  (perch or red snapper)
1 bunch cilantro, with roots
1 stalk lemon grass
1 galangal root
6 fresh Kaffir lime leaves
2 cups coconut milk
2 cups stock
1 fresh banana flower
3 to 4 large chilies
fish sauce, to taste
lime juice, to taste

FISH & SEAFOOD

FRIED MAHI MAHI WITH WATERCRESS
Pla Phaboong

Keep fish filets whole or cut into bite-sized pieces. Coat with fish sauce. Refrigerate until ready to use. Separate watercress into three bunches. Mince shallots and garlic. Rinse soybean seeds to remove salt. Finely slice chili.

Stir-fry shallots, garlic, soybeans and chili in hot oil. Add watercress and cook, stirring often. Season with desired balance of fish sauce, oyster sauce, light soy sauce and sugar. If desired, add stock to thin and create a sauce.

Dredge filets in flour, shaking off any excess. In a wok or deep skillet fry in hot vegetable oil until crisp. Drain on paper towels.

To serve, arrange filets in sauce and serve immediately.

• 112 •

1 3/4 lbs. fresh mahi-mahi
   filets (or other ocean fish)
fish sauce, to taste
1 1/4 lbs. Chinese watercress
3 to 4 shallots
3 to 4 garlic cloves
1 tbsp. soybean seeds
1 large fresh chili
2 tbsp. peanut oil
fish sauce, to taste
oyster sauce, to taste
light soy sauce, to taste
sugar, to taste
stock, if needed
flour
vegetable oil for frying

FRIED FISH WITH CELERY

Pla Phat Dongoong Chai

Peel and thinly slice ginger root and soak in salt water for 1 hour. Keep fish filets whole or cut into bite-sized pieces, coat with fish sauce and refrigerate. Rinse soybean seeds well. Slice celery, mushrooms and spring onions into bite-sized pieces. Set each vegetable, including soybeans seeds, soaking in separate bowls of water.

Mince shallots. Thinly slice chilies and garlic. Sauté garlic slices in oil until golden brown. Set aside for later garnish. In a mortar or garlic press, crush cilantro roots together with peppercorns. In a wok or skillet, sauté both in 1 teaspoon oil until their full aroma is released. Add shallots and drained celery, mushrooms, onions, and ginger root and brown well. Add soybean seeds and chilies. Stir in stock and season with desired balance of soy sauce, fish sauce and sugar. Bring to a boil, then reduce heat and simmer. Thicken sauce to desired consistency with tapioca flour.

Dredge filets in flour, shaking off excess and fry in hot vegetable oil until golden brown. Drain on paper towels. Serve filets with vegetables in their sauce or with sauce on the side. Garnish with reserved garlic.

• • • • • • • • • • • • • •

1 young ginger root
1 3/4 lbs. ocean fish filets
fish sauce, to taste
1 tbsp. soybean seeds
4 to 5 ribs celery
4 oyster mushrooms
2 to 4 spring onions or scallions
3 to 4 shallots
3 to 4 large Thai chilies
2 to 3 garlic cloves
1 tbsp. peanut oil
2 to 3 cilantro roots
1 tbsp. whole peppercorns
1 tsp. peanut oil
3/4 cup stock
light soy sauce, to taste
fish sauce, to taste
sugar, to taste
tapioca flour
white flour
vegetable oil for frying

• 113 •

FRIED MINCED FISH FINGERS

Thod Man Pla

Purée fish filets. Cut long beans into thin rings. Roll up lime leaves and cut into thin slices. Mix puréed fish, beans and lime leaves together. Add eggs and, depending on desired spiciness, chili paste. Season with fish sauce and thicken with a little flour. Form oblong patties from fish mixture and fry in hot peanut oil until golden brown.

1 1/3 lbs. ocean fish filets
10 to 14 yard-long beans
3 to 4 fresh Kaffir lime leaves
3 eggs, beaten
1 to 2 tbsp. chili paste
fish sauce, to taste
white flour
peanut oil for frying

STIR-FRIED SQUID IN GARLIC & CHILI

Pla Muk Phat Prik Bai Krapao

Rinse each squid thoroughly under cold, running water. Peel skin and discard along with tentacles, head and innards. Remove and discard transparent cuttlebone. Rinse remaining bodies thoroughly, cut each in half and place flat on a cutting board. With a sharp knife, score a large cross-cut into each squid piece.

Sauté basil leaves in 1 tablespoon hot oil, remove and drain on paper towels. Coarsely chop half of the garlic cloves and fry in same oil until golden brown. Set basil and fried garlic aside for later garnish. Thinly slice shallots. In a mortar or garlic press, crush chilies and remaining garlic. Sauté resulting paste in remaining oil. Add green pepper, shallots and squid and briefly stir-fry. Season with desired balance of fish sauce, soy sauce, oyster sauce and sugar. Thin with stock if necessary. Serve with a garnish of reserved fried basil and garlic.

1 3/4 lbs. young squid
3 to 4 sprigs of Thai basil
3 tbsp. peanut oil
3 to 4 garlic cloves
1 to 2 shallots
3 to 4 large Thai chilies
2 to 3 small Thai chilies,
1 tbsp. chopped green bell pepper
fish sauce, to taste
light soy sauce, to taste
oyster sauce, to taste
sugar, to taste
1/4 to 1/3 cup stock

STUFFED FRIED SQUID

Pla Muk Yud Sai

Rinse each squid thoroughly under cold, running water. Peel skin and discard along with tentacles, head and innards. Remove and discard transparent cuttlebone. Rinse remaining bodies thoroughly and leave whole for filling.

Shell prawns, halve lengthwise and devein. Purée prawns together with fish filets. Crush cilantro roots in a mortar. Add to purée and blend well, seasoning with desired balance of soy sauce and pepper. Mince desired amount of chiles and add. Spoon mixture into the squid, close and secure with kitchen string. Steam squid over low heat for 10 minutes, then fry in vegetable oil until golden brown.

To prepare sauce, mince chilies and spring onions and slice garlic into thin strips. Mix in fish sauce and lime juice.

Serve squid with salad greens, accompanied by sauce on the side.

• • • • • • • • • • • • • • •

4 fresh young squid
6 oz. prawns
6 oz. Dover sole or sea bass filets
3 cilantro roots
light soy sauce, to taste
freshly-ground pepper, to taste
fresh Thai chilies, to taste
vegetable oil, for frying

• • • • • • • • • • • • • • •

SAUCE:
3 to 4 Thai chilies
3 to 4 spring onions or scallions
2 to 3 garlic cloves
2 tbsp. fish sauce
1 tsp. lime juice
fresh seasonal salad greens

• 115 •

Fried Squid with Garlic & Vegetables

Pla Muk Kratiem Prik Thai Phak Ruom

Rinse each squid thoroughly under cold, running water. Peel skin and discard along with tentacles, head and innards. Remove and discard transparent cuttlebone. Rinse remaining bodies thoroughly, cut each in half and place flat on a cutting board. With a sharp knife, score a large cross-cut into each squid piece.

Mince half of the garlic cloves. Place squid in a marinade of soy sauce, pepper, and half of the minced garlic. Set aside until ready for use. Slice remaining half of the whole garlic cloves into thin strips and sauté in oil until golden brown. Set aside for later garnish.

Peel broccoli stems and slice on the diagonal. Coarsely chop broccoli leaves. Roughly chop cabbage. In hot oil, sauté broccoli leaves, stems and cabbage with remaining half of minced garlic. Season with desired balance of oyster sauce, fish sauce and sugar.

Remove squid from marinade and dust lightly with flour. Fry in vegetable oil until golden brown. Drain on paper towels. To serve, arrange sautéed vegetables on a serving platter, top with squid and garnish with reserved garlic.

● ● ● ● ● ● ● ● ● ● ● ● ●

1 1/2 lbs. fresh young squid
6 to 8 garlic cloves
light soy sauce, for marinade
freshly-ground pepper
1 tbsp. peanut oil
4 to 6 stems Chinese broccoli
1 Chinese cabbage
2 tbsp. peanut oil
oyster sauce, to taste
fish sauce, to taste
sugar, to taste
peanut oil, for frying
white flour
vegetable oil, for frying

FISH & SEAFOOD

CRAYFISH IN CHILI-BASIL SAUCE

Saus Prik Goong Talay

● ● ● ● ● ● ● ● ● ● ● ● ●

Separate crayfish meat from shells, keeping shells as intact as possible. Rinse shells, pat dry and fry in 1 tablespoon hot oil. Drain on paper towels and set aside.

In a mortar or garlic press, crush together chilies and garlic. Thinly slice shallots and fry briefly in remaining oil. Add chili-garlic paste and sauté well. If necessary, add stock to thin. Season with desired balance of fish sauce, soy sauce, sugar and pepper.

Coat crayfish meat with fish sauce, dust with flour and fry in vegetable oil until golden brown. Drain on paper towels. To serve, return crayfish meat to their shells. Add basil leaves to sauce just before spooning over crayfish.

1 1/2 lbs. crayfish
2 tbsp. peanut oil
desired mix of 6 to 8 small and large chilies
4 to 6 garlic cloves
3 shallots
1/4 to 1/3 cup stock
fish sauce, to taste
soy sauce, to taste
sugar, to taste
freshly-ground pepper, to taste
white flour
2 tbsp. vegetable oil
1 bunch Thai basil leaves

• 118 •

FISH & SEAFOOD

FRIED PRAWNS

Goong Thod

halve prawns in shells lengthwise and devein. Season with fish sauce and dust with flour. Fry in vegetable oil over low heat until golden brown. Serve with any sauce, like *Chili-Basil Sauce* (page 118), *Ginger Sauce* (page 106) or *Panaeng Curry Paste* (page 147).

● ● ● ● ● ● ● ● ● ● ● ●

1 1/2 lbs. prawns
fish sauce, to taste
white flour
vegetable oil, for frying

MASHED FISH WITH RICE NOODLES & VEGETABLES

Khanom Chin Nahmya Pla

trim off and discard tips of galangal root. Roughly chop galangal root together with krachai root and lemon grass. Thinly slice shallot and chilies. Mince garlic. Combine ingredients in a pot, add fish filets and water and simmer over low heat until cooked through. Carefully remove fish and spices and let cool. Strain stock and reserve.

In a mortar, crush fish and spices into a purée. Heat coconut milk and stir in fish purée and reserved stock. Season with desired balance of fish sauce and sugar.

In a separate pot, cook rice noodles in unsalted boiling water. Transfer to a colander, then plunge into cold water. Drain noodles and arrange on a platter. Top with sprouts, basil and beans and serve with hot purée and a garnish of dried chiles.

● ● ● ● ● ● ● ● ● ● ● ●

1 galangal root
1 krachai root
2 stalks lemon grass
1 shallot
fresh large chilies
3 to 4 garlic cloves
1 to 2 perch filets, depending on size
1/2 cup water
3/4 cup coconut milk
fish sauce, to taste
sugar, to taste
1 package rice noodles
soy bean sprouts, to taste
Thai basil leaves, to taste
yard-long beans, to taste
dried chilies, for garnish

Goong Thod

FISH & SEAFOOD

OCEAN PERCH WITH GREEN RICE

Pla Khao Mao

Cut fish filets into medium-sized pieces. In a mortar, crush together garlic cloves and peppercorn. Blend in enough soy sauce, making sure amount of marinade will cover filets. Marinate filets for 15 minutes.

Combine eggs and lime juice. Lightly flour filets, dip into egg mixture and coat with rice. Fry filets in oil until golden. Serve with *Chili-Basil Sauce* (page 118), *Ginger Sauce* (page 106) or *Panaeng Curry Paste* (page 147).

• • • • • • • • • • • • •

1 1/2 pounds ocean perch filets
3 to 4 garlic cloves
1 tablespoon peppercorns
light soy sauce
2 eggs, beaten
1 teaspoon lime juice
white flour
1 to 2 cups cooked green rice
vegetable oil, for frying

PRAWNS IN SOYBEAN SAUCE

Goong Kratiem Prik Thai

Shell prawns, halve lengthwise and devein. In a mortar, crush together cilantro roots, garlic cloves, peppercorns, then mix in 2 tablespoons of the oil. Cover prawns with marinade and set aside for 30 minutes. Briefly stir-fry soybean sprouts in remaining oil. Season with desired balance of soy sauce, oyster sauce, fish sauce and sugar.

Remove prawns from marinade (reserve marinade), dust with flour and fry in vegetable oil until golden. Drain on paper towels. Remove soybean sprouts from sauce, arrange on a platter and top with prawns. Mix leftover prawn marinade with soybean sauce and finely-sliced garlic clove, if desired, Cook briefly, then pour over prawns. Garnish with reserved cilantro leaves.

• • • • • • • • • • • • •

4 to 8 prawns
2 to 3 cilantro roots with leaves reserved for garnish
6 to 8 garlic cloves
1 tablespoon peppercorns
3 tbsp. peanut oil
1 pound soybean sprouts
light soy sauce, to taste
oyster sauce, to taste
fish sauce, to taste
sugar, to taste
flour
vegetable oil for frying
1 garlic clove (optional)

Pla Khao Mao

FISH & SEAFOOD

PRAWN KABOBS WITH RICE-STUFFED PINEAPPLE HALVES

Khao Phat Supparot Goong

Shell prawns, halve lengthwise and devein. Slide each prawn half onto a wooden skewer, then coat with fish sauce. Set aside. Cut pineapple lengthwise, trim off leaves and remove pulp from skin. Dice into small pieces. Chop cucumber, bell pepper and shallot. Crush cilantro root in a mortar. Mince garlic and fry in 1 tablespoon oil until golden brown.

In a wok or skillet, stir-fry cilantro root with cucumber, red pepper and shallot in remaining oil. Add egg and blend well. Add pineapple and fried garlic. Season with desired balance of fish sauce, sugar and pepper. Add cooked rice and blend.

Dust skewered prawns with flour and fry in oil until golden brown. Drain on paper towels. To serve, warm the hollow pineapple halves and fill with rice mixture. Accompany with skewered prawns and *Panaeng Curry Paste* (page 147).

4 to 8 prawns
fish sauce, to taste
1 pineapple
1/2 cucumber
1/2 red bell pepper
1 shallot
1 cilantro root
2 to 3 garlic cloves
1 tbsp. peanut oil
1 egg, beaten
sugar, to taste
freshly ground pepper, to taste
4 to 6 cups cooked rice
flour
vegetable oil, for frying

FISH & SEAFOOD

Nested Prawns, Squid & Chicken

Ba Mee Kratong Goong, Pla Muk Gai

Soak egg noodles in cold water until ready to use. Shell prawns, halve lengthwise and devein. Rinse each squid thoroughly under cold, running water. Peel skin and discard along with tentacles, head and innards. Remove and discard transparent cuttlebone. Rinse remaining bodies thoroughly, cut each in half and place flat on a cutting board. With a sharp knife, score a large cross-cut into each squid piece. Set aside.

Roughly chop broccoli leaves and stir-fry in oil until crisp. Drain and set aside for later garnish. Cut chicken breast into large bite-sized pieces. Slice oyster mushrooms and spring onions. Mince garlic.

Drain noodles well. To create noodle nests: using a special two-part baking sieve, distribute noodles evenly throughout the bottom and sides of larger sieve, then press the second, smaller sieve against them to form a nest. Carefully dip the secured sieves into enough hot oil to cover. Keep smaller sieve in place until noodles are fried. Carefully remove hot noodles and drain on paper towels. Make a total of 4 nests.

Stir-fry chicken pieces in 2 tablespoons oil, adding mushrooms, scallions, garlic and, lastly, the prawns and squid. Fry until golden brown. Add stock and season to taste with chili sauce and fish sauce. If mixture becomes too thin, thicken with tapioca flour. Divide seafood mixture equally into noodle nests and garnish with reserved broccoli leaves.

- 8 oz. egg noodles
- 4 to 6 prawns
- 4 young squid
- 4 to 6 leaves Chinese broccoli
- 5 oz. boneless, skinless chicken breast
- 2 to 3 oyster mushrooms
- 4 to 6 spring onions or scallions
- 3 to 4 garlic cloves
- peanut oil, for deep-frying
- 2 cups stock
- chili sauce, to taste
- fish sauce, to taste
- tapioca flour, if necessary

FISH & SEAFOOD

PRAWNS WITH SATOW BEANS

Goong Satow

Shell prawns, halve lengthwise and devein. Coat prawns with fish sauce. Set basil leaves soaking in water until ready for use. Remove seeds from satow bean pods, rinse well and cut in half. Pick leaves off cilantro stems and set aside. In a mortar, crush together cilantro roots and garlic cloves. Finely slice chilies.

In a wok or skillet stir-fry satow beans in oil. Add cilantro-garlic mixture and chilies and continue cooking. Season with desired balance of fish sauce, soy sauce and sugar.

Dust prawns with flour and fry in vegetable oil until golden brown. Drain on paper towels.

Just before serving, mix basil and cilantro leaves with beans, arrange on platter and top with prawns.

● ● ● ● ● ● ● ● ● ● ● ● ●

8 to 12 prawns
fish sauce, to taste
2 sprigs Thai basil leaves
4 to 5 satow bean pods
2 to 3 cilantro roots with leaves
3 to 4 garlic cloves
3 to 4 large Thai chilies
1 tsp. peanut oil
light soy sauce, to taste
sugar, to taste
flour
vegetable oil for frying

PRAWNS WITH RICE NOODLES

Gwaytiao Phat Thai Goong

Soak noodles in cold water until soft. Drain. Cut spring onions into 1-inch pieces. Slice cabbage into thin strips. Finely chop peanuts. Mince garlic. Thinly slice chilies and cover with vinegar to marinate.

Fry garlic in a wok or deep skillet Add noodles, spring onions, cabbage, soybean sprouts and eggs. Season with desired balance of fish sauce, soy sauce, sugar and lime juice.

Shell prawns, halve lengthwise and devein. Coat prawns with fish sauce and fry in vegetable oil until golden brown. Drain on paper towels. Set aside.

To serve, arrange prawns over rice noodles and garnish with chopped peanuts. Accompany dish with marinated chilies and lime halves on the side.

• • • • • • • • • • • • • •

1 package of rice noodles
6 to 8 spring onions or scallions
1/2 small white cabbage
1 tbsp. fresh unsalted peanuts
3 to 4 garlic cloves
2 to 3 large Thai chilies
1/3 cup white wine vinegar
2 tbsp. peanut oil
6 oz. soybean sprouts
2 eggs, slightly beaten
fish sauce, to taste
light soy sauce, to taste
sugar, to taste
lime juice, to taste
4 to 8 prawns
vegetable oil, for frying
lime halves, for garnishing

PRAWNS WITH GINGER & MARINATED GARLIC

Goong Sohn King

Shell prawns, halve lengthwise and devein. Season with fish sauce and set aside until ready to use. Combine 2 tablespoons fish sauce, lime juice and sugar and heat briefly until sugar dissolves. Set aside to cool.

Peel and thinly slice ginger root. Finely slice marinated garlic, chilies and scallions.

Blanch prawns in boiling water and drain. To serve, arrange on a platter alongside fresh greens, sprinkling both with cooled sauce. Serve ginger, marinated garlic, chilies, scallions, peanuts and cilantro leaves as accompaniments.

• • • • • • • • • • • • • •

1 3/4 lbs. prawns
fish sauce, to taste
2 tbsp. fish sauce
2 tbsp. lime juice
1 tbsp. sugar
1 young ginger root
3 heads marinated garlic,
   (store-bought)
3 to 4 large chilies
6 to 8 spring onions or scallions
seasonal salad greens
2 tbsp. fresh unsalted peanuts
1 bunch cilantro leaves

• 130 •

STIR-FRIED PRAWNS & EGGPLANT

Khao Phat Gaeng Kiew Wan Goong

Quarter eggplants, reserving small chopped amount for later garnish. Thinly slice chilies. Roll up lime leaves and slice into thin strips.

Shell prawns, halve lengthwise and devein. Sauté curry paste in oil until full aroma is released. Gradually stir in coconut milk, stirring constantly. Add eggplants and lime leaves. Add prawns and continue cooking, stirring constantly.

When prawns are cooked through, add rice and mix well. Add chilies and season with desired balance of fish sauce and sugar. Heat through thoroughly. To serve, arrange on a serving platter and garnish with basil, sliced eggs and reserved eggplant.

● ● ● ● ● ● ● ● ● ● ● ● ● ●

6 Thai eggplants, stems cut
3 to 4 large chilies
2 to 3 fresh Kaffir lime leaves
8 to 12 prawns
1 to 2 tbsp. green curry paste
2 tbsp. peanut oil
3/4 cup coconut milk
4 to 6 cups cooked rice
fish sauce, to taste
sugar, to taste
1 to 2 sprigs Thai basil
hard-boiled eggs, for garnish

PRAWNS IN GARLIC SAUCE

Goong Kratiem

Shell prawns, halve lengthwise and devein. Mince half of the garlic cloves and fry in oil until golden brown. Thinly slice the remaining cloves.

Combine fried garlic with desired balance of fish sauce and light and dark soy sauces. Add half of stock and bring to a boil. Thicken with tapioca flour. Let cool, then add prawns and marinate for 15 minutes. Remove prawns from marinade and fry with sliced garlic in vegetable oil until golden brown. Drain on paper towels. Add remaining stock to marinade and bring to a boil. Pour over prawns and serve garnished with sliced onions and finely-sliced chilies.

● ● ● ● ● ● ● ● ● ● ● ● ● ●

4 to 8 prawns
3 to 4 garlic cloves
1 tbsp. peanut oil
fish sauce, to taste
light soy sauce, to taste
dark soy sauce, to taste
3/4 cup stock
tapioca flour
vegetable oil for frying
spring onions or scallions, for
   garnish
chilies, for garnish

Vegetables

Vegetables are featured frequently on Thai menus not only because Buddhist teaching calls for vegetarianism, but also because vegetables are inexpensive and abundant throughout Thailand. A Thai vegetable platter is a feast for the eyes. This is because Thais are masters of presentation and rarely do vegetables reach the table untouched and in their original form. For example, chili pods can be lightly scored, dipped in ice water, and—lo and behold—emerge in the form of a pagoda. After being submerged in ice water, multiple incisions made to the stalk ends of spring onions turn into luscious, crinkly, green curls. Whether entwined, knotted, carved into leaves or rolled, most vegetables are served with *nahm prik*, the spicy sauce that uniquely enhances the taste of even the dullest vegetable.

The palette of Thai vegetables can sometimes be a source for confusion, however. Many have familiar Western names but look entirely different. Chinese broccoli consists of long stems and leaves. Yard-long beans can, indeed, measure up to a yard long. Cucumbers are slightly rounder in shape, while eggplants can have a variety of appearances—green, yellow, white, striped, long, round or egg-shaped.

Don't be frustrated if at first you fail to achieve the same results found on festively decorated Thai tables. Vegetable carving can be very intricate. Advanced techniques are taught in Thai schools of higher education. Even some homes in Thailand employ chefs whose sole job is to carve ordinary vegetables into works of art. It is only important to remember that these sculptures have an ancient, royal heritage and aim to reflect the elements found in the very soul of Thailand: patience, harmony and beauty.

SHAOM

Khai Shaom

Remove leaves from shaom, beginning at the bottom and working your way to the top, taking care to avoid thorns. Mince garlic and fry in lightly-oiled wok or skillet until golden brown.

Toss shaom with eggs and garlic, season with soy sauce and fish sauce. Cook shaom-egg mixture in hot oil like an omelet until golden brown on both sides. Pat away excess oil with paper towels. Cut omelet into bite-sized pieces and serve. This vegetable dish is also delicious cold.

• 134 •

● ● ● ● ● ● ● ● ● ● ● ● ● ● ●

1 lb. shaom
3 to 4 garlic cloves
peanut oil, for frying
2 eggs, beaten
light soy sauce, to taste
fish sauce, to taste

SATOW BEAN STIR-FRY

Phat Prik King Satow

Rinse bean seeds well and cut in half lengthwise. Mince shallots, slice chilies into thin rings and cut scallions into 1–inch pieces. Mince garlic and fry in 1 tablespoon oil until golden brown.

Sauté curry paste in remaining until full aroma is released. Add bean seeds, shallots and chilies and stir-fry. Stir in desired amount of stock. Add scallions and garlic. Season with desired balance of fish sauce and sugar. Arrange on serving platter and serve immediately

● ● ● ● ● ● ● ● ● ● ● ● ● ● ●

14 oz. shelled satow beans
2 shallots
2 small chilies
4 to 6 spring onions or scallions
4 garlic cloves
2 tbsp. peanut oil
1 to 2 tbsp. red curry paste
stock, to taste
fish sauce, to taste
sugar, to taste

STIR-FRIED EGGPLANT

Phat Makua

Trim off and discard the tops of eggplants. Blanch in boiling, salted water. Remove, cool, then cut into bite-sized pieces. Coarsely chop shallots and mince garlic. Thinly slice oyster mushrooms. Slice chilies on the diagonal into thin rings.

In a wok or deep skillet, stir-fry eggplant in oil until skin is nice and crisp. Transfer to platter and keep warm. In the same pan, stir-fry shallots, garlic and chilies. Add mushrooms. Season to taste with pepper, sugar and fish sauce. If desired, add stock to thin. Spoon sauce over eggplant and serve immediately.

• • • • • • • • • • • • • • • • • •

4 to 6 long eggplants
1 to 2 shallots
3 to 4 garlic cloves
3 to 4 oyster mushrooms
1 to 2 small chilies,
2 tbsp. peanut oil
freshly-ground pepper, to taste
sugar, to taste
fish sauce, to taste
1/4 to 1/3 cup stock, to thin

• 135 •

Stir-Fried Thai Vegetables

Phat Phak Ruom

Rinse vegetables and cut into bite-sized pieces. Slice chilies on the diagonal into thin rings. Slice shallots. Mince garlic and fry in a lightly-oiled wok until golden brown. Set aside.

In a wok or deep skillet, stir-fry vegetables by adding them in order of firmness, starting with the firmest-fleshed vegetables first. Add shallots and chilies and continue frying to desired tenderness. Season with desired balance of fish sauce, oyster sauce, soy sauce, and sugar. Stir in stock and fried garlic. Arrange on a serving platter and serve immediately.

• • • • • • • • • • • • •

9 to 12 oz. fresh Thai vegetables:
eggplant, beans, broccoli, satow
beans, Chinese watercress, or
soybean sprouts
1 to 2 small chilies
1 to 2 shallots
6 to 8 garlic cloves
peanut oil
fish sauce, to taste
oyster sauce, to taste
light soy sauce, to taste
sugar, to taste
3/4 cup stock

Stir-Fried Vegetables with Prawn Sauce

Nahm Prik Kra Pi

Crush garlic cloves in a mortar. Add shrimp paste and blend well. Thinly slice eggplants and chilies and add. Continue crushing together until a paste forms. If too thick, dilute with water. Season with desired balance of fish sauce, lime juice and sugar.

Cut vegetable mix into bite-sized pieces and either fry, steam, or serve raw with prawn sauce on the side. Vegetables can also be accompanied by fried seafood, such as shrimp, scallops, or squid.

• • • • • • • • • • • • •

4 to 6 garlic cloves
1 to 2 tsp. shrimp paste
1 to 2 Thai eggplants
small and large chilies, to taste
1/4 cup water, if needed
fish sauce, to taste
lime juice, to taste
sugar, to taste
9 to 12 oz. mixed Thai vegetables:
eggplants, bamboo, shaom, Chinese
cabbage, or yard-long beans

Nahm Prik Kra Pi

VEGETABLES

DESSERTS

The Thai symphony of culinary delectables ends in an adagio amabile—dessert. Bewitching perfumes emanate from ripe fruits. Artistically carved, their aroma and form make them seductive. The meat of the most royal of fruits, the delectable mango, has a cream-like consistency that, when enhanced by sticky rice, is sheer ecstasy. A close second to the mango is the irresistible red papaya with its mild-tasting meat. The mangosteen fruit hides its marvelously fragrant meat inside an unadorned shell. The rambutan, related to the litchi, is nearly as white on the inside. Bananas grown in Thailand are sweet and scented. Rarely eaten raw, they are baked, fried, or deep fried. The durian fruit is an acquired taste. One must get beyond its overripe cheese odor and through a prickly rind to reach a thoroughly satisfying and creamy white meat.

Thailand's wealth of native fruits provides a natural refreshment to the country's sometimes relentless heat. Thais also favor extremely sweet and extra-rich desserts as a counterbalance to the spiciness of a meal. Street vendors sell dessert snacks similar to those offered by other oriental cuisines. Other desserts conform more closely to Western conventions, and often incorporate the ubiquitous coconut. These include *Rice Balls in Coconut Sauce,* the highly-esteemed *Sticky Rice with Fresh Mango,* or *Pumpkin Filled with Coconut Milk Custard*—all wonderful ways to bring a marvelous Thai meal to a close.

STICKY RICE WITH FRESH MANGO

Khao Niew Mamuang

Steam rice and keep warm until ready for use. Combine coconut milk with sugar and salt in a wok or large saucepan and heat slowly until sugar dissolves. Add warm rice, blend well, then let stand for 30 minutes.

To serve, peel and slice mangoes and arrange on a platter with rice.

• • • • • • • • • • • • • • •

1 cup sticky rice

3/4 cup coconut milk

2 to 3 tablespoons palm sugar

1 teaspoon salt

4 ripe mangoes

RICE BALLS IN COCONUT SAUCE

Khao Mao Klug

Combine water and salt, add rice and soak until soft. Drain rice well. Break coconut in half, reserving milk. Finely chop coconut meat. Mix together rice, coconut meat and sugar. Form small balls from mixture, arrange in a steamer and steam 20 to 30 minutes.

Using a whisk and beating briskly, blend reserved coconut milk with desired amount of sorbet. Spoon sauce onto plates and decorate with rice balls.

• • • • • • • • • • • • • • •

3/4 cup water

1 teaspoon salt

1/4 cup green rice

1 coconut

2 tablespoons palm sugar

sorbet (recipe on page 148)

Khao Niew Mamuang

DESSERTS

PUMPKIN FILLED WITH COCONUT MILK CUSTARD

Sahngkayah Fahk Tong

Cut off top third of pumpkin and remove seeds. Beat eggs until foamy, then fold in palm sugar, salt and coconut milk. Pour into mixture into pumpkin and steam for 30 to 45 minutes, or until pumpkin is tender. Cool thoroughly, then slice like a pie.

Complement this dish with coconut sorbet or any other fruit sorbet (recipe page 148).

• • • • • • • • • • • • • • •

1 pumpkin (about 2 pounds)
4 eggs
2 to 3 tbsp. palm sugar
1 tsp. sea salt
2 cups of coconut milk

BAKED BANANAS

Gluay Klug

Prepare a batter from flour, egg, melted butter, sugar and salt. Peel bananas and cut into bite-sized pieces. Dip banana pieces into honey, then into batter. Fry immediately in hot oil. Serve alone or with sorbet.

• • • • • • • • • • • • • • •

3/4 cup flour
1 egg
1 tbsp. melted butter
1 to 2 tsp. palm sugar
1/2 teaspoon sea salt
4 to 6 Thai bananas
2 tbsp. honey
peanut oil for deep-frying

Gluay Klug

DESSERTS

Ponlamai Thai: Carved Exotic Fruit

DESSERTS

BASICS

Curry pastes are best prepared in a mortar. However, if you do use a food processor, use very low speeds. Curry pastes can be prepared in advance and kept refrigerated for about a week. Divide larger quantities into portions and freeze.

Red Curry Paste

Soak large and small chilies in lukewarm water for 1 hour. Drain well. Toast cumin and coriander seeds in a skillet without oil. Cool. Mince garlic and finely slice shallots. In a mortar, combine all ingredients and crush to form a paste, mixing in shrimp paste last. Refrigerate until ready to use.

• •

10 large dried chilies
10 small dried chilies
1/2 teaspoon cumin
1/2 teaspoon coriander seeds
30 garlic cloves
2 to 3 shallots
1 tablespoon finely-sliced galangal root
1 teaspoon finely-sliced Kaffir lime peel
1 teaspoon salt
1 teaspoon shrimp paste

Green Curry Paste

Soak small, dried chilies in lukewarm water for 1 hour. Drain well. Finely slice yellow and green chilies. Set aside. Toast cumin and coriander seeds in a skillet without oil. In a mortar combine all ingredients and crush to form a paste, mixing in shrimp paste last. Refrigerate until ready to use.

• •

10 small dried chilies
10 fresh yellow chilies, seeded
20 to 30 small green chilies
1/2 tsp. cumin
1/2 tsp. coriander seeds
1/2 tsp. salt
1 tsp. finely-chopped galangal root
1 tsp. peppercorns
1 tbsp. finely chopped cilantro root
1 tsp. finely sliced lemon grass
1 tsp. finely-sliced Kaffir lime peel
15 to 20 garlic cloves
2 to 3 shallots
1/2 teaspoon shrimp paste

Panaeng Curry Paste

Soak large and small chilies in lukewarm water for 1 hour. Drain well. Toast coriander seeds, cumin and peanuts in a skillet without oil. Mince garlic cloves and shallots.

In a mortar, combine all ingredients and crush to form a paste, mixing in shrimp paste last. Refrigerate until ready to use.

10 large dried chilies
15 small dried chilies
1/2 tsp. coriander seeds
1/2 tsp. cumin
2 to 3 tbsp. fresh unsalted peanuts
30 garlic cloves
1 to 2 shallots
2 tsp. peppercorns
1/2 tsp. salt
1 to 2 tsp. finely-chopped galangal root
1 to 2 tsp. finely-sliced lemon grass
1 tsp. finely-sliced Kaffir lime peel
1 to 2 tsp. finely-chopped cilantro root
1/2 tsp. shrimp paste

Massaman Curry Paste

Soak chilies in lukewarm water for 1 hour. Drain well. Finely dice chilies. Cut lemon grass, cilantro and galangal roots into thin strips. Mince garlic and shallots and stir-fry in oil. Remove from skillet.

Toast lemon grass, cilantro and galangal roots in skillet. Stir in shrimp paste along with remaining ingredients and blend. Place mixture in a mortar and process into a paste. Refrigerate until ready to use.

7 to 10 large dried chilies, seeded
1 stalk lemon grass
2 to 3 cilantro roots
1/2 galangal root
5 garlic cloves
3 shallots
2 tsp. peanut oil
1 tsp. shrimp paste
1 tsp. ground cardamom
1 tsp. salt
1 tsp. Ceylon cinnamon
1 tsp. cumin

Sorbet

Combine fruit purée with sugar. Add juice and water. Bring to a boil and cook until sugar thermometer reads 180 degrees. Cool and freeze in a sorbet freezer.

1 quart fruit purée
1 cup sugar
juice of 1 lime or lemon
1 quart water

Beef stock is the preferred stock for recipes in this book, since since beef bones impart a stronger and more distinct flavor to Thai dishes. However, if you prefer not to use beef bones when preparing stock, you may substitute chicken or lamb bones, or, in the case of seafood dishes, fish bone.

Stock

In a large dutch oven, bring beef bones and water to a boil and simmer over low heat for about 6 hours, routinely skimming off fat. Final stock should be clear, and if not, may be strained through cheesecloth.

Note: If you must use ready-made broths, be sure they do not contain any salt or other aromatics.

2 lbs. beef bones
5 quarts water

Source List

For ingredients & kitchenware:

A. J.'s Finest Foods
7141 East Lincoln Drive
Scottsdale, AZ 85253
602-998-0052

Anzen
736 Martin Luther King Blvd.
Portland, OR 97232
503-233-5111

The Chile Shop
109 E. Water Street
Santa Fe, NM 87501
505-983-6080

Chinese-American Trading Co.
91 Mulberry Street
New York, NY 10013

The CMC Company
PO Drawer 322
Avalon, NJ 08202
800-262-2780

Dean & Deluca
560 Broadway
New York, NY 10012
212-226-6800

Hot Stuff Spicy Food Store
PO Box 2210
New York, NY 10039
212-254-6120
800-Want Hot

Jensen's Market
102 South Sunrise Way
Palm Springs, CA 92262
619-325-8282

La Cusine
323 Cameron Street
Alexandria, VA 22314
703-836-4435
800-521-1176

Le Saucier
Faneuil Hall Marketplace
Boston, MA 02109
617-227-9649
FAX: 617-424-0132

Mo Hotta-Mo Betta
PO Box 4136
San Luis Obispo, CA 93403
805-544-4051

Nancy's Specialty Market
PO Box 327
Wye Mills, MD 21679
800-462-6291

The Oriental Pantry
423 Great Road
Acton, MA 01720
508-264-4576
800-828-0368

Pendery's
1221 Manufacturing
Dallas, TX 75207
214-741-1870
800-533-1870

Spice Merchant
PO Box 524
Jackson Hole, WY 83001
307-733-7811

Strawbridge & Clothier
801 Market East
Philadelphia, PA 19107
215-629-6000

Thai Kitchen/Epicurean
International
PO Box 13242
Berkeley, CA 94701
510-268-0209
FAX: 510-834-3102

William Sonoma
1-800-541-1262

For plants & seeds:

The Cook's Garden
PO Box 535
Londonderry, VT 05148
802-824-3400

De Giorgio Seeds
6011 N Street
Omaha, NB 68117-1634
402-731-3901
800-858-2580

Nichols Garden Nursery
1190 North Pacific Hwy
Albany, OR 97321
503-928-9280

Sandy Mush Herb Nursery
316 Surrett Cove Road
Leicester, NC 28748
704-683-2014

Seeds of Change
3209 Richards Lane
Santa Fe, NM 87505
505-438-8080

• 149 •

RECIPE INDEX

RECIPE TITLES IN ENGLISH
● ● ● ● ● ● ● ● ● ● ● ● ● ● ● ● ● ● ●

Salads

Egg Noodle Salad with Pork-Stuffed Broccoli
    Leaves, 50
Fresh Oyster Salad, 38
Fresh Squid Salad, 36, *37*
Glass Noodle Salad, 44, *45*
Large Mixed Salad, 51
Papaya and Prawn Salad, 46, *47*
Prawn Salad, 32, *33*
Sautéed Chicken and Vegetable Salad, 39
Sautéed Pork Salad, 48
Seafood Salad with Pork, 40, *41*
Sliced Beef Salad, 48, *49*
Sour Mango Salad with Crayfish, 34, *35*
Spicy Chicken Salad, 42, *43*
Spicy Tuna Salad, 38

Soups

Chicken and Coconut Soup, 58, *59*
Coconut Soup with Mussels, 61
Coconut Soup with Prawns and Potatoes, 64
Egg Noodle Soup with Puréed Chicken, 60
Ginger Soup with Red Snapper, 66, *67*
Glass Noodle Soup with Chicken, 56, *57*
Lemon Grass Soup with Vegetables, 64
Prawn Soup with Lemon Grass, 54, *55*
Rice and Ginger Soup, 62, *63*

Curries

Green Curry with Beef, 70, *71*
Green Curry with Fresh Coconut, 70
Massaman Curry with Chicken, 72, *73*
Panaeng Curry with Prawns, 78, *79*
Red Curry with Beef and Krachai Root, 76, *77*
Red Curry with Chicken and Yard-Long
    Beans, 74
Red Curry with Chicken, 74, *75*
Red Curry with Steamed Chicken, 72

Meat and Poultry

Beef with Egg Noodles and Vegetables, 86, *87*
Beef with Fried Rice Noodles and Chinese
    Broccoli, 84, *85*
Chicken in Fried Rice with Yard-Long Beans
    and Basil, 98
Chicken with Satow Beans, 92, *93*
Deep-Fried Chicken Tenders with Ginger
    Sauce, 102
Eggplant Stuffed with Red Beef Curry, 90, *91*
Fried Chicken-Corn Patties, 92
Marinated Chicken in Pandan Leaves, 96, *97*
Marinated Chicken Wings, 102, *103*
Sautéed Beef with Krachai Root, 82, *83*
Stir-Fried Beef with Cashews, 88, *89*
Stir-Fried Chicken with Bamboo, Asparagus
    and Oyster Mushrooms, 101
Stir-Fried Chicken with Chilies and
    Basil, 94, *95*
Stir-Fried Chicken with Chinese Broccoli and
    Ginger, 99
Tomatoes Stuffed with Chicken, 100

Fish and Seafood

Fish in Coconut Sauce, 110, *111*
Fried Crayfish in Chili-Basil Sauce, 118, *119*
Fried Fish with Celery, 113
Fried Mahi Mahi with Watercress, 112
Fried Minced Fish Fingers, 114
Fried Ocean Perch with Green Rice, 122, *123*
Fried Prawns, 120, *121*
Fried Prawns with Garlic, 131
Fried Rice with Green Curry and Prawns, 131
Fried Squid with Garlic and Vegetables,
    116, *117*
Mashed Fish with Rice Noodles and
    Vegetables, 120
Nested Prawns, Squid and Chicken, 126, *127*
Ocean Fish Filet and Ginger Sauce, 106, *107*
Prawn Kabobs with Rice-Stuffed Pineapple
    Halves, 124, *125*
Prawns in Soybean Sauce, 122
Prawns with Ginger and Marinated
    Garlic, 130
Prawns with Rice Noodles, 129
Prawns with Satow Beans, 128
Steamed Fish with Chicken and Chinese
    Cabbage, 108, *109*
Stir-Fried Squid in Garlic and Chili, 114
Stuffed Fried Squid, 115

Vegetables

Satow Bean Stir-Fry, 134
Shaom, 134
Stir-Fried Eggplant, 135
Stir-Fried Thai Vegetables, 136
Stir-Fried Vegetables with Prawn Sauce, 136

Desserts

Baked Bananas, 142, *143*
Carved Exotic Fruit, *144*
Pumpkin Filled with Coconut Milk
    Custard, 142
Rice Balls in Coconut Sauce, 140
Sticky Rice with Fresh Mango, 140, *141*

Basics:

Green Curry Paste, 146
Massaman Curry Paste, 147
Panaeng Curry Paste, 147
Red Curry Paste, 146
Sorbet, 148
Stock, 148

RECIPE TITLES IN THAI:
● ● ● ● ● ● ● ● ● ● ● ● ● ● ● ● ● ● ●

Salads

Bah Mee Jok Kwahn Dong, 50
Lahb Gai, 42, *43*
Som Tam Goong, 46, *47*
Yum Gai Yang, 39
Yum Goong, 32, *33*
Yum Goong Talay Mamuang, 34, *35*
Yum Hoy Naerng Rom, 38
Yum Moo Nam Tok, 48
Yum Moo Talay, 40, *41*
Yum Neua, 48, *49*
Yum Pla, 38
Yum Pla Muk, 36, *37*
Yum Woon Sen, 44, *45*
Yum Yai, 51

• 151 •

Soups

Khao Tom Gai King, 62, *63*
Tom Gaeng Chud Woon Sen, 56, *57*
Tom Kha Gai, 58, *59*
Tom Kha Hoy Lay, 61
Tom Kha Man Farang Goong, 64
Tom Mee Sah, 60
Tom Yum Goong, 54, *55*
Tom Yum Khamin Pla Soth, 66, *67*
Tom Yum Mangsawirat, 64, *65*

Curries

Gaeng Gai Nah Mai, 74, *75*
Gaeng Kiew Wan Neua, 70, *71*
Gai Phat Prik King Tuafang Yiew, 74
Gai Pim, 72
Goong Panaeng, 78, *79*
Maprao Ohn Song Kruang, 70
Massaman Gai, 72, *73*
Neua Phat Prik Bai Krachai, 76, *77*

Meat and Poultry

Ba Mee Laht Nah Neua, 86, *87*
Bik Gai Thod Kratiem Prik Thai, 102, *103*
Gaeng Phat Neua Yud Sai Ma Kua, 90, *91*
Gai Grob Piew Wan, 102
Gai Phat Hoy Bai Toy, 96, *97*
Gai Phat Nah Mai Falang, 101
Gai Phat Phak Khanah King, 99
Gai Phat Prik Bai Krapao, 94, *95*
Gai Satow, 92, *93*
Gai Thod Khao Phod, 92
Khao Phat Gai Bai Krapao, 98
Makeua Teht Daengna Sod Sai, 100
Neua Phat Krachai, 82, *83*
Neua Phat Met Mamuang, 88, *89*
Phat Siya Neua, 84, *85*

Fish and Seafood

Ba Mee Kratong Goong, Pla Muk
    Gai, 126, *127*
Goong Kratiem
Goong Kratiem Prik Thai, 122
Goong Satow, 128
Goong Sohn King, 130
Goong Thod, 120, *121*
Gwaytiao Phat Thai Goong, 129
Khanom Chin Nahmya Pla, 120
Khao Phat Gaeng Kiew Wan Goong, 131
Khao Phat Supparot Goong, 124, *125*
Pla Hao Mok, 108, *109*
Pla Khao Mao, 122, *123*
Pla Muk Kratiem Prik Thai Phak
    Ruom, 116, *117*
Pla Muk Phat Prik Bai Krapao, 114
Pla Muk Yud Sai, 115
Pla Phaboong, 112
Pla Phat Dongoong Chai, 113
Pla Phat King Soth, 106, *107*
Pla Tom Yum Khati, 110, *111*
Saus Prik Goong Talay, 118, *119*
Thod Man Pla, 114

Vegetables

Khai Shaom, 134
Nahm Prik Kra Pi, 136, 137
Phat Makua, 135
Phat Phak Ruom, 136
Phat Prik King Satow, 134

Desserts

Gluay Klug, 142, *143*
Khao Mao Klug, 140
Khao Niew Mamuang, 140, *141*
Ponlomai Thai, 144
Sahngkayah Fahk Tong, 142

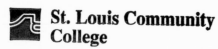

GYPSIES

GYPSIES

PHOTOGRAPHS BY
JOSEF KOUDELKA
AN APERTURE BOOK

Aperture, Inc.,
publishes a Quarterly of Photography, portfolios, and books to communicate
with serious photographers and creative people everywhere.
Subscriptions to the Quarterly are available at $17.50 for four issues.
A catalog of publications is available upon request.
Photographs copyright © 1975 by Josef Koudelka. Historical text copyright ©
1975 by Willy Guy.
Published in the United States by Aperture, Inc.,
Elm Street, Millerton, New York 12546, and simultaneously in France
by Robert Delpire Editeur, Paris; in Great Britain
by Gordon Fraser Gallery, Ltd., London;
and in Canada by Gage Trade Publishing, Agincourt, Ontario.
Library of Congress Catalog Card Number 75–13611
ISBN 0–912334–74–6
ISBN 0–912334–85–1 Museum Edition
The book has been prepared and designed by Robert Delpire and
produced by Aperture, Inc.
Manufactured in the United States of America.
Printed by Rapoport Printing Corporation and bound by Publishers Book Bindery.
2 4 6 8 9 7 5 3
First Printing

Josef Koudelka's photographs aim at a visual distillation of a pattern of human values: a pattern that involves theater, large gesture, brave style, precious camaraderie and bitter loneliness. The pattern and texture of his pictures form the silent equivalent of an epic drama.

Koudelka's pictures seem to concern themselves with prototypical rituals, and a theater of ancient and unchangeable fables. Their motive is perhaps not psychological but religious. Perhaps they describe not the small and cherished differences that distinguish each of us from all others, but the prevailing circumstance that encloses us.

John Szarkowski
Director, Department of Photography
The Museum of Modern Art

At first Koudelka was attracted by the physical beauty of the gypsies of Eastern Europe, the strangeness of their movements and their facial expression, by their clothing and ornaments; later he was attracted by their life-style. In the end he was completely absorbed by his subject.

He developed a great feeling for the Gypsies; drawn to them, he sought to learn the origin of those things which first attacted him. He worked constantly to get to know them better, in depth, in order to establish profound contacts. He devoted himself to his subject with burning intensity.

Koudelka achieves restraint and clarity, and a respect for human beings. His work reflects a long evolution of his vision from the external to the inherent and ultimate nature of his subjects.

Anna Fárová
Prague, Czechoslovakia

The photographs published in this book
were taken mostly in the separated Gypsy settlements in East Slovakia
during the period 1962–1968.

Zehra. 1967

Vinodol. 1968

Vinodol. 1968

Vinodol. 1965

Okres Nove Zamky. 1967

Rakusy. 1964

Velka Lomnica. 1966

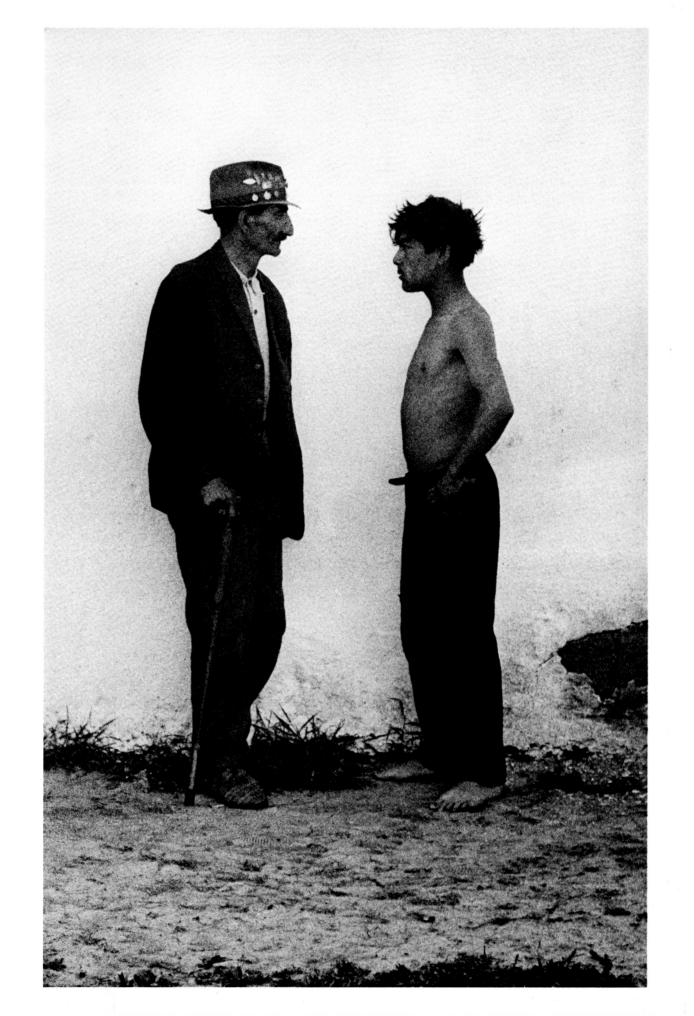

Velka Lomnica. 1963

Utekac. 1963

Bardejov. 1967

Velka Lomnica. 1963

Okres Galanta. 1965

Poprad. 1963

Spisske Bystre. 1966

Svinia. 1966

Giraltovce. 1966

Jarabina. 1963

Bardejov. 1967

Jarabina. 1963

Velka Lomnica. 1966

Zehra. 1967

Kadan. 1963

Jihlava. 1967

Velka Lomnica. 1966

Zehra. 1967

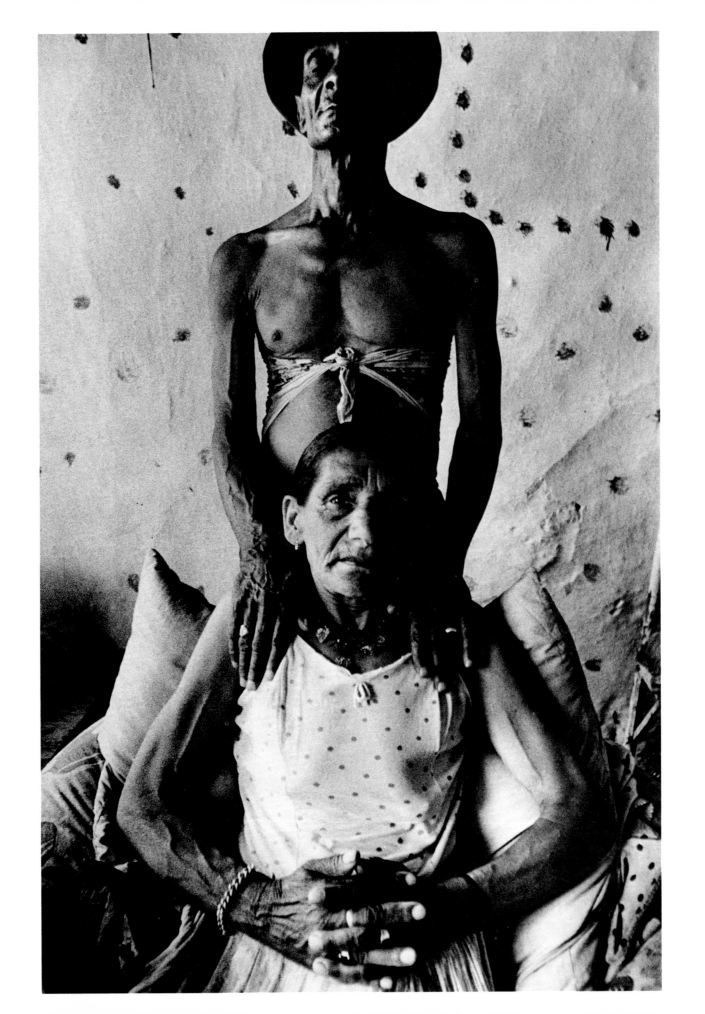

Okres Spisska Nova ves. 1966

Bratislava. 1962

Velka Lomnica. 1963

Bratislava. 1965

Kendice. 1965

Kadan. 1963

Podhorany. 1967

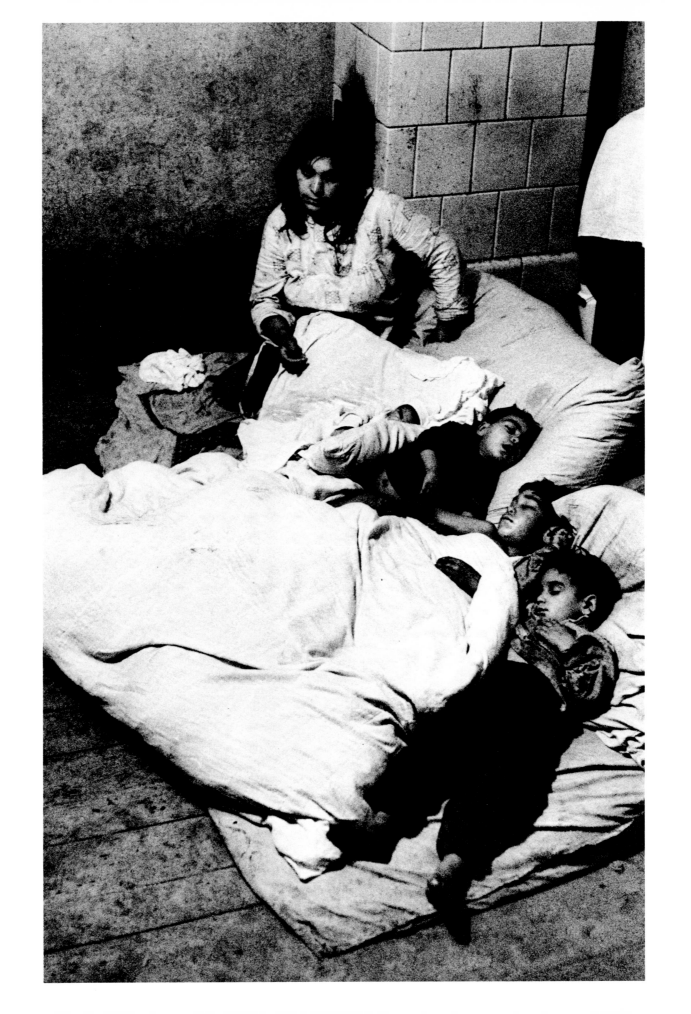

Okres Hnusta. 1967

Straznice. 1965

Cierny Balog. 196*

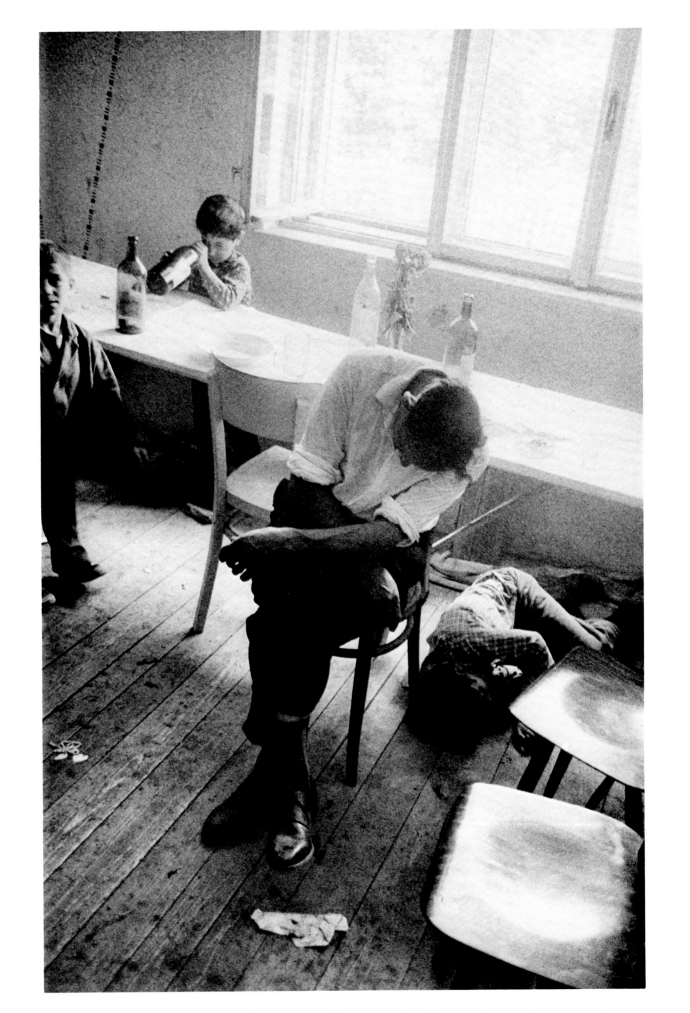

Kadan. 1962

Svinia. 1966

Rakusy. 1963

Teplice. 1967

Kadan. 1963

Velka Lomnica. 1966

Kadan. 1963

Okres Poprad. 1963

Okres Roznava. 1968

Zehra. 1967

Michalovce. 1965

Okres Bardejov. 1966

Okres Roznava. 1968

Spisske Bystre. 1967

Podhorany. 1967

Okres Poprad. 1967

Rakusy. 1964

Klenovec. 1967

Jihlava. 1967

Bardejov. 1967

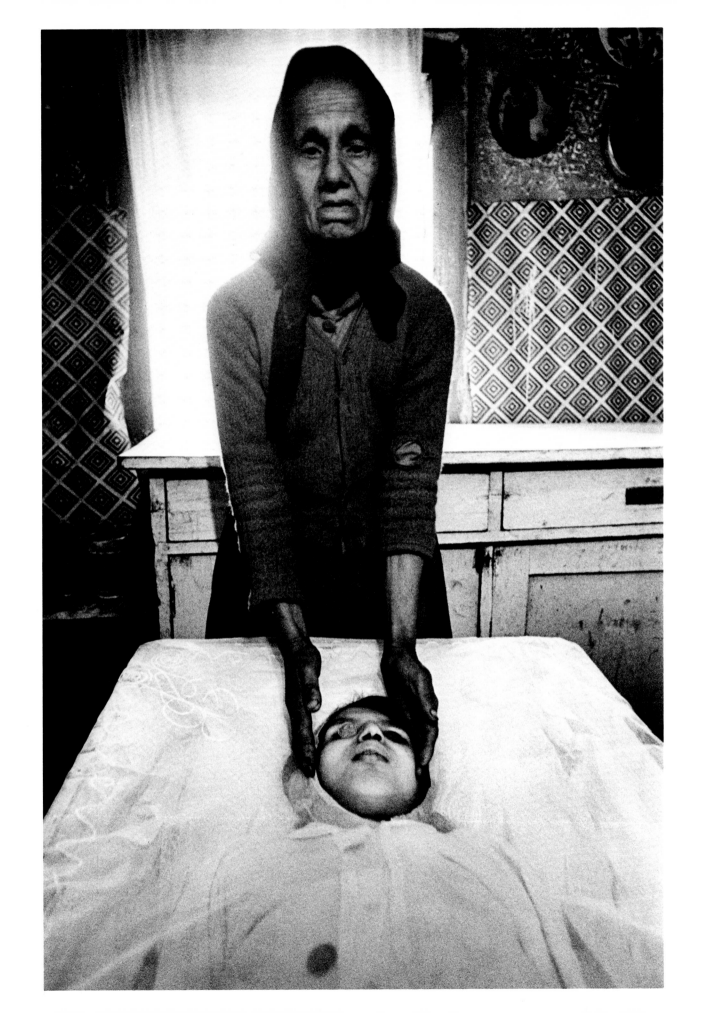

Jarabina. 1963

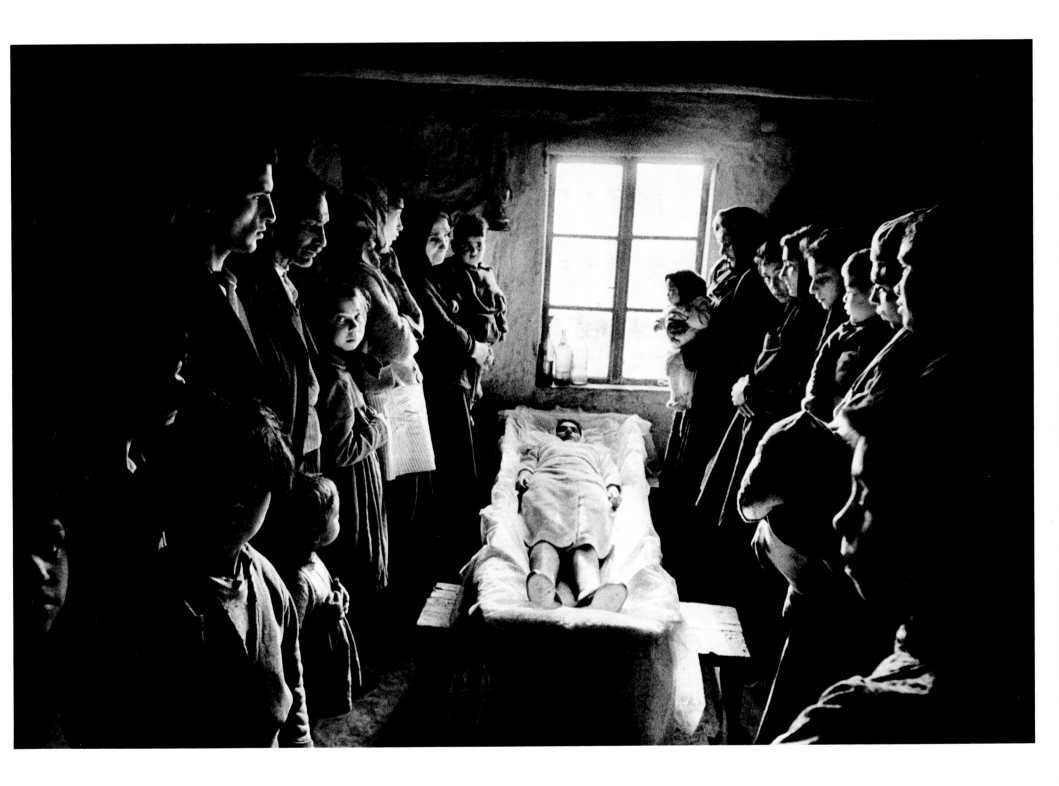

The Gypsies left their original homeland in northern India around 1000 A.D. This much has been established by historical and linguistic research, but the reason for their exodus westward is not known. They reached Europe by the early fourteenth century, crossing from Asia Minor by way of Crete and the Peloponnesus, and continued their dispersion westward and northward.

By the end of the fourteenth century they were already settled in large numbers in the Balkans and Danube lands, where an undeveloped economic structure and primitive technology gave Gypsy smiths and cobblers the chance to compete with local artisans. Rulers soon incorporated the newcomers into their social and economic order by permitting them to work and imposing taxes or by simply making serfs of them.

The early history of the Gypsies in Western Europe is strikingly different. In 1417 a remarkable group, several hundred strong, appeared in Hungary. After traveling westward across Slovakia and Bohemia (hence the French name for Gypsy, *bohémien*), the large company divided into groups which were later to appear in Germany, Switzerland, Italy, France and northern Spain. In the guise of penitents on a pilgrimage of expiation these groups aroused the attention of Western Europe, partly because of their unusual appearance but also because they were supported by impressive letters of safe-conduct from the Holy Roman Emperor and even the Pope. The Gypsy bands made their livelihood by soliciting alms, performing magic, telling fortunes, buying and selling horses, and petty thieving—all occupations compatible with or even requiring nomadism.

Early accounts of their arrival suggest that the curiosity and sympathy they originally aroused were accompanied by suspicion and hostility, and soon their status changed dramatically from protected guests to persecuted outlaws. Within a hundred years of the first appearance of the Gyp-

sies, most countries in Western Europe had passed savage laws for their expulsion; some even legislated to include the death penalty.

Present-day Czechoslovakia, consisting of Bohemia, Moravia and Slovakia, straddles the frontier of what could be called the western and eastern areas of Gypsy history in Europe. To the west, in the Czech lands of Bohemia and Moravia, the pattern of development has been similar to that in Germany, France and England: the approach of the government toward Gypsies usually has been to ignore them as worthless, or to legislate expulsion and execution in order to deter further immigration. In Western Europe, Gypsies are still largely nomadic to this day.

However, in Slovakia, the eastern part of the Republic, the pattern resembles that of the Danube lands and the Balkans. Gypsies were often seen as potentially valuable and from their first appearance were permitted, encouraged and even forced to settle. It is here that we still find the largest numbers of Gypsies, mainly settled although some groups have remained nomads.

The first legislation against Gypsies in Bohemia followed the outbreak of fires in Prague in 1541, when they were suspected of acting as paid incendiaries of Turkish invaders. From this time onward, there was periodic legislation in a vain effort to drive Gypsies from the Czech lands, culminating in serious attempts to exterminate them as a group in the troubled century following the Thirty Years' War (1618–48). Gypsies were slaughtered and their mutilated corpses hung from trees along the border. Later, warning signs bearing the symbol of the gallows appeared. In the Czech lands, signs proclaimed that hanging awaited all Gypsies entering the country; in Slovakia the warning was tempered by a promise of amnesty for those who agreed to settle within three weeks of passing the border.

It was only with the Age of Enlight-

enment in the eighteenth century that outright persecution of the Gypsies ceased throughout the Hapsburg Empire. As part of a general endeavor to transform their realm into a rational centralized state, Empress Maria Theresa and then her successor, Joseph II, hoped to turn all Gypsies into productive workers by assimilating them into the peasantry. In 1758, the Imperial Governors' Council, which was charged with preparing and supervising the program, issued the first of numerous edicts that Gypsies still traveling should seek a master and settle, while those already living in isolated huts and tents should be admitted to the serfs' villages. Local authorities were required to demolish their former dwellings and build new houses for them, without any recompense from the Imperial Exchequer. In addition they were expected to reemploy Gypsies in normal occupations, especially in public works such as road-building and ditching. The Gypsies' new masters were to beat them if they worked badly and were instructed to take particular care that they "wasted no time on music."

So that Gypsies should not slip back into their former way of life, they were prohibited from taking to the roads, returning to their previous dwelling places, and dealing in or owning horses — but to ensure their total assimilation even more extreme measures were prescribed. They were forbidden to wear outlandish clothes and speak the Romany language; where there were doubts that the children would receive a disciplined and Christian upbringing, their offspring were to be taken by force and placed in foster homes with farmers or apprenticed to craftsmen. To mark the change—that Gypsies no longer existed as such—they were renamed *Neubauern* (new farmers) or *Ujmagyar* (new Hungarians).

By the time the policy lapsed with the death of Joseph II in 1790, little had apparently changed. In the Czech lands most of the Gypsies continued to wander as they had before, although numbers of Gypsies had abandoned their traveling life in Slovakia. There, the majority of Gypsies had long been settled—at the outskirts of villages or near feudal castles—and on the whole they remained in their huts, the men working as smiths, musicians or farm laborers, the women as domestic servants.

The assimilation attempt failed, partly because of understandable Gypsy resistance to settling on such harsh terms but more significantly because of widespread administrative sabotage by equally resistant local authorities. These saw negligible benefits to themselves in disbursing their own precious funds on Gypsies and consequently often ignored edicts and even falsified census returns by which the Imperial Governors' Council assessed their performance.

During the nineteenth century little attention was paid to the Gypsies, although the nomadic groups in Czech lands were looked upon as nuisances and were required to make their presence known by registering with the authorities, as they were in other countries of Western Europe at that time. Meanwhile, the clusters of huts in Slovakia grew steadily into larger settlements.

Following the First World War the new Czechoslovak Republic recognized Gypsies as a separate nationality in 1921. This was an empty gesture, however, as it made no difference to their situation, which was desperate after the long period of wartime privation. In the same year the Slovak Peasants' Union complained that "since they have nothing, the Gypsies either beg or steal and as poverty cases they are a burden on the peasantry." The authorities of a district in East Slovakia complained of difficulties in controlling Gypsies, for ". . . the penalty of imprisonment has no effect on them, because imprisonment only improves their living conditions. It often happens that a Gypsy without resources commits a crime only to escape the pangs of hunger."

The general economic depression between the wars only worsened relations between Gypsies and other Czechoslovak citizens. In 1927 a law was passed that permitted nomadism only with the sanction of the police and local authorities, who could withdraw it at any time without reason. No alternative employment or accommodation was provided for those who were refused a pass. One year later a pogrom in West Slovakia claimed the lives of six Gypsies, including two young children, in reprisal for pilfering crops from the fields. A popular daily newspaper commented, "The case can be characterized as a citizens' revolt against Gypsy life. . . . The Gypsy element, such as it is today, is really an ulcer on the body of our social life which must be cured in a radical way." The court apparently concurred and proceeded to sentence the murderers to only sixteen months' imprisonment. Such outbreaks of popular violence against Gypsies were not confined to Czechoslovakia; during the same period, pogroms occurred in Austria, Germany and France.

These events were merely a prelude to the horror of the Second World War, when the Nazis placed Gypsies high on their list of racial and national minorities to be eliminated. Their intention to purge Europe of Gypsies by progressive stages is evident from the spreading annihilation. First to perish were the Gypsies in Germany, where their fate had already been prepared in the years before the war. Then came Gypsies in territories occupied by the German army and finally those in friendly states. Nazi race theorists proposed that one or two groups of Gypsies should be exempted—for study purposes—but eventually even these few were not spared.

Although the war did not develop in the way the Nazis had planned, nevertheless over a quarter-million Gypsies perished at their hands. Most Gypsies in the Czech lands, a German protectorate, shared the fate of German Gypsies and almost vanished as a distinct group in the gas chambers of the concentration camps.

The far more numerous Gypsies of Slovakia were fortunate by comparison under the autonomous puppet state that had been established there. In some areas they were ordered to move their huts further away from towns and villages, and where they already lived in houses among non-Gypsies they were forced to abandon their homes and build new isolated settlements. Gypsies were permitted to visit towns only on specified days at fixed times and were completely excluded from cinemas, restaurants, parks and public transport.

Still, though some men were sent to forced-labor camps and Slovak fascists occasionally raided Gypsy settlements, beating their inhabitants and in a few cases burning them alive in their huts, there was no mass extermination. The war had ended too soon for that.

With the promise of the postwar Communist-led government that discriminatory practices would not be tolerated, thousands of Gypsy families left the settlements in which they had been virtually imprisoned for centuries to seek work in industrial areas of the Czech lands. For the first time in history Gypsies entered the general labor market in large numbers, usually as unskilled construction or factory workers. While the government grudgingly approved this mass migration as "a positive response to their new opportunities," it was noted that whether in cities, settlements or on the road Gypsies still lived a separate life —partly self-sought, partly imposed on them.

In the Czech urban areas Gypsies formed what were becoming virtually minor ghettos, clearly visible by the mid-1950's. The situation in Slovakia was little better, for the departure of the migrants had only momentarily checked the growth of the settlements. There, numbers were swelled by the high birth rate as well as by families returning home from the Czech lands who had seen their stay as a temporary expedient—to earn the high wages that were not to be had locally. Meanwhile, groups of traditionally nomadic Gypsies, called Vlachs, still traveled the country in their horse-drawn carts, more or less free from any control.

This continuing segregation was viewed with alarm by policy-makers since it perpetuated what they termed "the old primitive Gypsy way of life with all its bad habits." Gypsies were regarded as outmoded — an anachronism incompatible with the new social order. As in the time of Maria Theresa, no positive value was seen in preserving their separate identity; this was to be eliminated as rapidly as possible by dispersing them, thus destroying their social life and bringing them into contact with "progressive" non-Gypsy patterns. Assimilation was said to be in the Gypsies' own interest.

In 1958, after some deliberation and even less research, the government launched an ambitious crash campaign to settle and assimilate Gypsies throughout the Republic. It was first necessary to gain control of the movement of Gypsies, and to achieve this a law was passed "on the permanent settlement of nomads." This law required that "local authorities shall provide comprehensive assistance to persons who lead a nomadic way of life to enable them to adopt a settled way of life; in particular they are obliged to help such persons in finding suitable employment and accommodation and by educational means to aim at making them orderly working citizens," and went on to warn that "whoever should continue in a nomadic way of life, in spite of having been offered help to settle permanently, will be punished for the offense by six months' to three years' deprivation of liberty." In fact, only the 6,000 ethnically distinct Vlachs, as well as a few surviving Czech Gypsy families, could properly be called nomads.

Local authorities, however, were instructed to interpret this term so broadly as to also include migrant Gypsies. The 20,000 entered on the register had their identity cards stamped and employers were told not to to release them without prior permission. In general, registered nomads were to be employed in the place where they had been registered, and despite the availability of transfers the government "did not expect the 'export' or 'import' of nomadic persons"—though this was to become overall policy a few years later. It was believed that this law would have the effect of halting migration, after which local authorities could carry out a planned dispersal of Gypsies by rehousing them away from their former concentrations, and it was even the hope that this dispersal might be completed within a decade.

The most instantly successful part of the campaign was in preventing the small yet significant proportion of true nomads from continuing their travels, bringing to an end in five brief days a traditional way of life which had survived in Czechoslovakia for as many centuries. Sometimes the nomads were given money for their horses, but in many cases these were simply taken away and slaughtered.

Housing for these now immobilized Gypsies varied enormously. For some it was nothing more than their own carts—with the wheels torn off—but well-intentioned officials moved others into new modern flats. The results were predictable, for these Gypsies were hostile to the idea of relinquishing their travels and naturally enough did their best to re-create an approximation of their former communal life around the campfire to draw some comfort from their unfamiliar surroundings. Such scenes did little to improve relations between newly settled Gypsies and their already unenthusiastic neighbors, who probably had themselves waited years for similar housing. As a report testified: "There are numerous complaints that Gypsies remove the stove from the kitchen to outside the house, where they later cook, using as fuel the flooring, door- and window-frames and sometimes even the rafters and ceiling, so that the house is soon uninhabitable." In the main, however, for the majority of "registered nomads" — that is, the non-Vlach migrant Gypsies—no rehousing was generally provided.

It soon became apparent that the campaign was failing on several counts. Czech employers, when in need of labor, were apt to turn a blind eye to the regulations and give jobs to "registered nomads" without seeking approval beforehand. In any case, local authorities had better things to do than attempting to keep track of their elusive charges. Consequently, there was no effective barrier to further migration, and "registered nomads" were joined by other Gypsies on their train journeys between home settlements in Slovakia and work places in the Czech lands. For the Vlachs, however, there was no return to the road, for a horse and cart would have been far too conspicuous and they generally remained where they had been trapped at the time of registration.

A more serious shortcoming was that the local authorities, especially in Slovakia, showed great reluctance to disperse Gypsies by allocating them either council flats or building plots outside the Gypsy settlements. Migrant Gypsies, on their return home with their savings, often had no choice but to build their new houses in the settlements, which frequently lacked electricity, adequate sanitation, and in some cases even drinkable water. Nor were local authorities eager to install such amenities, for the settlements were to be eliminated within a few years according to the overall plan. For the same reason potential builders among the Gypsies often were unable to get planning permission, and if they did build new family houses, local authorities were technically required to demolish them and fine or imprison the builders. In practice they tended to approve such "illegal" houses months or years after they had been built, but rather than run the risk more cautious Gypsies opted to build their familiar wooden huts instead.

A 1964 report from East Slovakia, the region with the largest Gypsy population in Czechoslovakia, revealed the extent of local authorities's lethargy. It was clear that the plan to eliminate all substandard settlements in the region by 1970 was out of the question, since only a dozen settlements had been demolished since 1958 while over four hundred remained. For the three-quarters of the region's 70,000 Gypsies who still lived in these settlements, conditions were actually deteriorating as their numbers grew. Particularly serious was the desperate lack of basic amenities. Each adequate well and toilet had to serve over two hundred Gypsies, and these conditions were reflected in infant mortality and TB rates of more than double the national average.

The government met to consider this critical situation and decided that the previous piecemeal approach to the problem of assimilation was inadequate. In 1965 the new plan was to disperse far more systematically than hitherto, and a special government committee was appointed to coordinate the action of local authorities throughout the republic. Effective dispersal was to be ensured by regular, planned transfers of Gypsies from what were termed "undesirable concentrations" to places with few Gypsies, which in practice meant from settlements in Slovakia to small towns and villages in the Czech lands. Other Gypsies were to be dispersed locally. At the same time the restriction on free migration, which had previously applied only to "registered nomads," was now extended to all Gypsies so that, in theory, only those Gypsies included in a planned transfer or dispersal were to be permitted to move; all other new migrants were to be sent home. As a

Gypsy spokesman laconically commented, "They plan how many there should be in each village: horses, cows and Gypsies."

To help in the decision as to which Gypsies should be transferred and dispersed, the government committee told the local authorities to classify them into three groups. In the first group were "those who no longer live in gypsy concentration . . . separated by only the final step from full assimilation." In the second were those who worked regularly, whose children attended school and who were "on the best road to escape from a gypsy environment." In the third and lowest group were

the most backward and wretched part of the gypsy population. They live a typical gypsy life in a gypsy concentration and as yet have no interest in leaving this concentration. If they work at all, they work irregularly, they do not send their children to school nor do they take much care of them and it cannot be said of them that they have attained any cultural level for they live in filth and from their numbers are recruited parasites and criminals. Among them are included many chronically ill or feeble people drawing sickness benefits who do not even want to be cured because their illness brings them an income without work. The solution of problems in assimilating gypsies from this group will be very demanding.

Those to be transferred and dispersed were to be chosen from the second group, the plan being to cream off the most adaptive Gypsies and spread them as thinly as possible throughout the republic, while the more intractable third group were to be left until later. In the meantime basic amenities in the settlements were to be improved.

How Gypsies were to be classified was left to arbitrary decisions of officials, and against these decisions the Gypsies had no

right of appeal. Indeed, they did not even have the right to be informed of their classification. As it turned out, this hardly mattered; the planned transfer system was effectively sabotaged by Czech local authorities who refused to accept their quotas, pleading that they had no free accommodation. The government committee's transfer timetable came to look more and more unrealistic as the percentage of planned transfers actually accomplished dropped from 85 percent in 1966 to only 20 percent in 1968. In all, less than 500 Gypsy families were transferred to the Czech lands in the three years the scheme was operative, while in the same period there were unplanned migrations of over double that number. Yet even if the plan had been completely fulfilled, the impact on the numbers in the still growing settlements would have been slight.

The scheme for transferring Gypsies finally collapsed in 1968 when the government, almost in desperation after ten years of failure in trying to disperse them, tentatively adopted the idea that better results might be achieved by allowing Gypsies to take a hand in planning their own future. Gypsy spokesmen, having been warned by the government in 1957 to abandon this idea, were at last given permission to form their own associations—one in the Czech lands and one in Slovakia. These grew swiftly, attracting not only the poorer Gypsies but the small and influential Gypsy intelligentsia which had been regarded as totally assimilated. Within two years these organizations were publishing their own magazines and promoting festivals of Romani song and dance, as well as arranging social functions. They provided a great stimulus for young Gypsy musicians, and soon pop groups began to appear on TV singing in Romani; they even reached the hit parade. Gypsies were increasingly referred to in the mass media as "Rom"—their own name for themselves—and this usage began to spread among the general public.

The promising experiment was short-lived. The associations were told to disband in 1973 on the stated grounds that they had "failed to fulfil their integrative function." The real reasons are harder to determine; probably among them are fears that the Gypsy associations would demand their privileges by right in claiming nationality status, disillusion with the confused finances of the associations, and general political changes since 1968.

Czechoslovakia today has one of the world's largest Gypsy populations—possibly even the largest if considered as a proportion of the country's total inhabitants. This minority has grown at a phenomenal rate, doubling in numbers over the past decade to more than a quarter of a million. Although they still formed less than 2 percent of Czechoslovakia's population, one child in eleven born there was a Gypsy.

Conditions are steadily improving for the one-third of the Gypsies living in the Czech lands, but a similar number still live in their old segregated settlements in Slovakia. Though the appearance of these settlements is changing gradually, this is due largely to the Gypsies' own efforts in building new brick houses; basic amenities are being installed with a painful lack of urgency, even though the government has long accepted that the settlements cannot be eliminated in the near future.

Since the war an increasing proportion of Gypsies have taken regular employment, and in 1970 the percentage for men reached the national average for the first time. The great majority, however, are unskilled and without educational qualifications. Consequently, Gypsy men from the predominantly rural settlements have the practical choice of working locally as relatively low-paid hands on the farms or in the woods or else traveling to urban areas, often in the Czech lands, to work in heavy-laboring gangs. Wages are much higher there, partly in recompense for the long hours of dirty, grueling work but also because such tasks as road-repairs and trenching are unpopular with the local work force. For the Gypsy family man with a home to make or maintain, the choice is simple yet not easy to make: remain at home where saving will be practically impossible, or leave his family behind in the hope of making something of a life in the future.

The other alternative—that of traveling with the whole family as in the postwar years — is now extremely difficult, because urban local authorities generally refuse to house or give residence permits to migrating Gypsy families — even in cases where they have already bought town apartments with their own money.

Some families still take the risk and squat in derelict houses scheduled for demolition, but most are daunted by the prospect of such a precarious existence. Meanwhile, in the barracks, where workers share bare and functional dormitories, there is no provision for families, and the occasional overnight visit from a wife can result in a stoppage from wages or even a dismissal.

The predicament of these Gypsies is not dissimilar to that of migrant workers in Western Europe, for, like them, they form an alien work force imported to do the most arduous and unpleasant jobs. Illiteracy is still a significant problem among adults, while children suffer badly at school from deficient knowledge of the languages used in teaching — Czech or Slovak. In many settlements Gypsy children hear almost nothing but Romani until they start school, for very few of them attend nursery school.

The future of Czechoslovakia's Gypsies is not easy to predict, but since over three-quarters of the children fail to complete their basic education it seems likely that this rising generation of Gypsies will be forced to repeat the experience of their parents.

Willy Guy